BEGINNING EDUCATOR

The fool doth think he is wise,
but the wise man knows himself to be a fool.

—*As You Like It* (5.1.30–31)

BEGINNING EDUCATOR

*Navigating
a Second Career
in Teaching*

Tim Clark

Bauhan Publishing
Peterborough New Hampshire
2022

ISBN 978-087233-355-0

Library of Congress Control Number: 2022905635
Information on file at the Library of Congress: www.loc.gov

Book design by Sarah Bauhan
Text set in Warnock Pro with Bodoni titles
Cover design by Joel Clark

Photos used by permission

BAUHAN
PUBLISHING LLC
PO BOX 117 PETERBOROUGH NEW HAMPSHIRE 03458
WWW.BAUHANPUBLISHING.COM   603-567-4430

Manufactured in the United States of America

For my grandchildren:
Annie, Sam, Charlie, Olive, Ellie,
and any others who may join them in the future

Foreword

"Beginning Educator": these are the words that are printed on the first teaching certificate a new teacher receives from the State of New Hampshire. The second certificate, and every renewal thereafter, says "Experienced Educator." When Tim became an "Experienced Educator" three years after he received his first certificate, he decided not to change the title of the twice-monthly columns he'd been writing for the *Monadnock Ledger-Transcript* newspaper, because he felt like a beginner still. He felt like a beginner throughout his teaching career, and for his whole life, he never stopped learning.

Tim taught for 13 years at ConVal High School, following a nearly 30-year career in journalism. He began this journey at 50, fairly set in his ways, used to the routines of a job he loved, and a touch arrogant about his ability to adjust to life in a public high school. He almost didn't make it through the first 12 weeks of school, but by March of his first year, he thought he might survive. I had begun teaching in the public schools three years before Tim did and had more experience in education, so I was able to coach him through some challenges. But in the long run, I think he helped me as much as I helped him.

One reason behind our success was that we almost always walked the dogs together when we got home in the afternoon from our respective schools. We talked a mile a minute during these walks, about our students, our struggles, our joys, our failures, and the state of public education. These walks, and the conversations we shared along the way, allowed us to reflect, analyze, strategize, and support each other through the best and worst of times. Often the thoughts we shared would make their way into Tim's column. Tim died before this book could be published, but he especially wanted his grandchildren to have it. He wanted them to know his thoughts, understand his experience, and be able to be close to him always. We, Tim's family, are delighted to share the essence of Tim with all of you.

—MAY CLARK

The Hardest Job

Ibecame an English teacher at ConVal High School in 1999 after 26 years as a journalist, the last 23 of them as an editor and writer at *Yankee* magazine in Dublin. Last week I decided to look at the diary I kept—intermittently—that first fall. Here are some of the early entries:

Sept. 6, Labor Day: Worked on planning for nine hours. Did no good at all. Didn't know what to plan. Graded profiles from American Lit.—not as good as I'd thought after first quick read. Terrible on commas.

Sept. 9: Another horrible week. I feel like we're at war, and they're winning. Ended on a low note Friday afternoon when I tried to read "The Monkey's Paw" out loud, in the dark, to my freshmen. So much noise I lost my temper, turned on the lights, quit reading. It was all coming from the same half-dozen kids, and the rest were probably enjoying the story. But I ruined it for them all.

Sept. 11–12: Worked eight hours Saturday, six Sunday. Powerful anxiety attack Sunday night, Monday morning. No sleep, no appetite. Told May Friday night that I knew what was bothering me. I'm working twice as hard for half the money, and I'm failing.

Sept. 18: I have lost seven pounds, most of it illusions.

Things got better, of course—I'm starting my third year now, the New Hampshire Department of Education has certified me as a "Beginning Educator," and I've gained back all that weight. But it's the hardest job I've ever done. It might be the hardest job there is.

This column is intended to tell you about a teacher's life. My life. It will be the kind of news that doesn't normally make the paper—hard questions about homework and grading and discipline, sure, but I'll try to avoid whining. I'd also like to put in funny stuff, like the boy that first year who, when I asked him to use the word "prosaic" in a sentence, said: "I forgot to take my prosaic this week." Or another boy in the same class who, after I defined "vacillate" as "to waver back and forth," came up with this gem: "After their team scored a touchdown, the crowd got up and vacillated." (9/20/01)

A Teacher's Funeral

Of all the reasons I decided to become a teacher, the most macabre was this: I wanted a teacher's funeral.

This was the result of attending the funeral for John Sullivan, a longtime ConVal High School English teacher who was killed in a bicycle accident the spring before I joined the faculty. The church was filled to overflowing with young people, students and former students of the tall, spare man with the wicked sense of humor who taught them about semicolons, sonnets, and Scott Fitzgerald. He taught them more than that, of course: Who would grieve over a semicolon?

I didn't know John, but my cubicle in the English office was once his. Ruth Ring, now retired, had the cubicle next to mine and helped me survive that hellish first year. She told me how John and Bob Fay, also now retired, used to play a game involving code numbers for jokes. For example, John would look over at Bob and say, "433!" Bob would guffaw and reply, "37!," and John would double over.

Ruth told me she once tried to get in on the act by singing out "477!" John and Bob looked at her, stone-faced, and then John turned to Bob and said, "Some people just don't know how to tell a joke."

Many of those at his funeral mentioned John's sense of humor, his fondness for puns, his gentle humanity. I looked around all those people and thought: Look at the lives he touched. Look at the difference he made. I edit a magazine that reaches two million readers. When I die, how many of them will weep for me? What difference have I made?

On September 21, I went to another memorial service, this one for my friend Bob LeBlanc, a University of New Hampshire geography professor who was on United 175 that awful day in New York City. The Johnson Theater was nearly full, but there weren't many of his students. They were where Bob had inspired them to go, scattered across the globe, studying distant places and distant cultures, pursuing careers—pursuing lives—in what Bob called "human geography." When the news of Bob's death found them, they sent a flood of emails back to remember and honor him. At one point, said Dean Marilyn Hoskin, emails about Bob were reaching the university website at a rate of one every 20 seconds.

One of them ended this way: "If any current UNH students are reading this, if you are struggling in a class and need help, go to your professor and talk to him or her. If you are lucky enough to have a teacher like Bob LeBlanc, you might just get that one tip, that one insight that will make it easier to succeed. You might learn something you will remember for the rest of your life."

When my time comes, I hope somebody will be able to say that about me. (10/4/01)

Emergency Plan

We had a faculty meeting the day after our third bomb threat in two weeks. Principal Sue Dell ditched the normal agenda so we could talk about our feelings. It was a difficult session. A lot of people were sad and angry about this homegrown terrorism. Teachers who had been around ConVal for a long time were mourning the death of an era in which we talked about lesson plans, not emergency plans. What happened?

One administrator suggested an answer. "We have a different socioeconomic profile," he said. "It's the haves and the have-nots. We have kids coming to school now with problems we couldn't imagine 20 years ago."

This is not news. For a long time, educational researchers have been saying that the main factor in academic success is economic status. There are individual exceptions, of course—poor kids who do very well and kids from wealthy families who couldn't care less. But mostly, the formula works: kids from rich families do better than kids from poor families.

You can see it most clearly in what some call the "digital divide," the gap between those with access to computers and those without. Last year, we were urged to email weekly progress reports to the parents of kids who were doing poorly. Guess what? Not one of my underperforming students had an email address. Some of them didn't have a telephone number.

When I teach my freshmen *Black Boy*, Richard Wright's devastating memoir of growing up poor in the Deep South, I ask them to write about a frightening experience from their pasts. Kids who get As and Bs usually describe the normal childhood terrors—scary dogs, getting lost at the mall, monsters under the bed. One girl wrote about sitting up in bed every night looking out the window, fearful that her parents would drive away and leave her.

Less successful students—the ones who struggle to read and write, who hate coming to school, who defy adult authority—write about death, divorce, drugs, and alcohol. They write about moving frequently and how hard it is to make new friends. They write about parents who really did drive away and leave them. They write about physical and sexual abuse—monsters in the bed, not under it.

"But this is Peterborough!" we say. "This is ConVal! It can't happen here!" I'm sure parents and teachers said the same thing in New Bedford and Springfield and Chelsea, Vermont, when horrific things happened. It can happen here. It can happen anywhere.

I don't worry about someone building an infernal device and smuggling it into ConVal. I worry about the ticking bombs who walk into school every morning without a shred of hope that they'll succeed. We need an emergency plan for them. (12/13/01)

The Other American Dream

Recently I wrote a letter of recommendation for a student in my Honors Freshman English class. We'll call him Joe Jones. It went to St. Paul's School and several other elite prep schools. I didn't send the following letter, but part of me wanted to.

Dear Admissions Committee:

I'm writing on behalf of Joe Jones. He's a terrific kid—a real leader in my class. He's smart, responsible, funny, energetic, creative, thoughtful, and popular with the other kids because he doesn't advertise his virtues. He's also been through a family tragedy, which has made him mature beyond his years. He'd be an outstanding member of your school community.

I hope you understand, however, if I have mixed feelings about writing this letter. I've been teaching Honors Freshman English for only two years, but this is the fifth kid I've recommended to you or other private schools like yours. They were all the kind of students a teacher dreams of having in a class. They force you to be a better teacher. They challenge you to be worthy of them, and the light in their eyes when you succeed makes you feel proud of yourself and your profession.

But you already know that. Your whole student body is made up of kids like these. And that's great, because not only do they benefit from your lovely and historic campus, your magnificent library, theater, and laboratories, and your distinguished faculty, they benefit from each other. Being around other remarkable students is an education in itself.

Still, I can't help feeling sad about losing them. I don't blame them or their parents for wanting the best—that's the American dream, isn't it? But there's another American dream, too—that we are all equal before God and the ballot box, and that fencing off our best and brightest youngsters from the rest of society is, in the long run, harmful to our democracy.

Public schools were invented with that second dream in mind.

Public schools are required to accept every student, regardless of his or her talents, intelligence, and family background. We may be the only nation on earth—the only nation in history—to believe that every child deserves an education and to attempt to give it to her or him. It's a magnificent ambition, and it's the source of most of our problems in public schools. We have to try to educate every student who walks in the door, no matter how deprived, damaged, disruptive, or dangerous he or she may be.

And we do it. We do it willingly, idealists or fools that we are. But teachers and administrators can't do it all by ourselves. We need kids like Joe, the kids other kids look up to and want to be like, to make this preposterous project feasible. We need them desperately. We need them more than you do. (1/17/02)

O Lord Methought What Pain

Bill Teunis was the first teacher I'd ever seen with a beard. It was the fall of 1965, and teachers with beards would soon become commonplace, but we didn't know that then. So when we walked into our sophomore English class at John F. Kennedy High School that September, we were startled by his appearance.

It wasn't just the beard. Most of our male teachers wore crew cuts, white dress shirts with skinny dark ties, black slacks, and polished black shoes, like FBI agents. In his tweed jacket worn over a denim work shirt—no tie—corduroy pants and brushed-leather desert boots, glowering at us over that bushy red beard, Mr. Teunis looked exotic and scary.

He may have dressed like an Ivy League student—in fact, he had recently graduated from Harvard—but he never tried to come on to us as a pal. If anything, he was stricter and more demanding than the men in the skinny ties. He was a tough grader. If you spelled the possessive "its" with an apostrophe, you automatically got an F. He tore my writing apart, splashing red ink around like a serial killer. He scolded me for being "coy," always holding up his beloved Hemingway as a model. "Don't be coy! Say what you mean! Fewer words!"

Mr. Teunis introduced me to Shakespeare. He loved to dress in Elizabethan garb and ham it up in class. His favorite speech was from *Richard III*:

> Oh lord, methought what pain it was to drown:
> What dreadful noise of water in mine ears!
> What sights of ugly death within mine eyes!

After I graduated, we began corresponding. In the spring of my sophomore year, I got a part in a play in Cambridge. I invited Mr. Teunis—I was never able to call him "Bill"—to come up and see me, and he accepted with pleasure. It must have been a few weeks after that letter came that I got a phone call from a high school friend.

"Have you heard about Mr. Teunis?" she said.

"No, what?"

"He drowned."

He and some of his students were swimming in the Shenandoah River, and one of the kids was swept into some rapids. Mr. Teunis dived in to save her. She made it back to shore. He never came up.

Someone once said that a writer should write for one person. I write for Mr. Teunis. (2/14/02)

Back in the Will

My mother always had high expectations for me. Once, when I was a teenager and resented all the pressure she put on me to succeed, she denied it. "You can be anything you want," she said. "A doctor, a lawyer, an architect." I don't recall the list including "a teacher."

It took her a while to accept managing editor of *Yankee* as a legitimate job (she thought if I had to be a journalist, I might as well be anchorman of the NBC *Evening News*), but when she did, she told me that she and Dad were taking me out of their will. I was doing fine, and my sisters needed the money more. I said that was okay with me.

I waited a long time before telling my mother about my decision to leave *Yankee* and become a teacher. I knew what she would say about it, but she always manages to surprise me with the way she says it. This time, she said nothing for a long minute. Then she said, "You're back in the will."

It could have been worse. A neighbor of mine in Dublin, I am told, learned of my decision and said, "He must have been canned. Nobody in his right mind would become a teacher." A colleague of mine in the ConVal English Department, who gave up teaching for a while, then went back, told me that a friend of his assumed he had come into an inheritance.

In last week's edition of *TIME*, there was a report that American elementary school teachers spend a billion dollars a year of their own money to buy additional supplies for their students. That's an average of $521 per teacher per year. First-year teachers, who are paid the least, spend the most, an average of $701 per year. "This profession attracts a special breed," the magazine quoted one expert. "Obviously they're not in it for the money."

She's right. And that's what made it all the more ironic a few weeks ago, when Federal Reserve Board Chairman Alan Greenspan said that public schools need to do a better job of teaching students "financial literacy." At first I was dismayed; then I laughed out loud. Teachers are the last people on earth who should be in charge of inculcating financial literacy. If we were financially literate, we wouldn't be teachers!

When I started this column, I promised to try to avoid whining. So here's all I want to say about the March 12 vote on a new teacher contract: How come everyone agrees that teachers are underpaid—until it's time to give them a raise? (2/28/02)

Thinking About Underwear

One of the Beat poets—Ferlinghetti?—wrote a poem that begins, "I've been thinking a lot about underwear." Well, we've been thinking a lot about underwear at ConVal High School lately. It's because we've come around to deciding that we need a dress code.

Some may be surprised that we don't have a dress code already. In a way, we do, but it's extremely vague—something about wearing "appropriate" clothing—and the result is that when the temperature goes up, we see a lot of clothing appropriate to spring break at Daytona Beach, only not as formal. I'm not sure why we're just getting around to something more rigorous, but it might be related to a workshop we had recently. When a lawyer told the faculty that, in the absence of a detailed dress code, a teacher who complains about the state of a student's dress, or undress, could be slapped with a complaint of sexual harassment, we all felt a little naked.

Hence the concern with underwear. According to the new rules, developed in consultation with some 400 students who attended open forums, there is to be no clothing that advertises drugs, alcohol, or tobacco use; expresses profanity, sexual innuendo, or violence; is ripped in inappropriate places; has protruding spikes; bares the back lower than the bra strap; or exposes cleavage anywhere.

The faculty met last week to go over the details. "Don't argue with students," Principal Sue Dell urged us. "Stick to the script!"

The script (written by Sue) tells teachers exactly what to say. "I believe you are in violation of our Dress Code," says Teacher. "Would you please add to or change your clothing?"

If Student is unwilling to do so, Teacher says, "If you cannot comply with my request, then I will have to send you to see an administrator."

Should Student continue to balk, Teacher is then to direct him or her to the office, calling ahead to specify the offense (visible bra strap, druggie hat, protruding spikes, cleavage frontal or dorsal).

The talk inevitably got raunchy, especially after one teacher, worried about consistency of enforcement, said, "I see cracks here that I don't want to see!" But the discussion exposed other kinds of cleavage as well. Does a Winston Cup auto racing T-shirt advertise tobacco products? Do the cleavage rules discriminate against girls who aren't fashionably skinny? Are parents aware that their daughters and sons come to school dressed like hookers or dope dealers? And if they are, what right have the schools to second-guess them?

I listened to the talk and didn't say much. The extravagance of adolescent mating plumage doesn't bother me, but I am prepared to enforce any rules we choose to make. Still, I can't escape the feeling that public schools inevitably reflect public values, and if we buy and sell clothing that we are ashamed to see on our children, then we have nobody to blame but ourselves. (4/25/02)

Bananas

Some decades ago, an economic advisor to the president warned that if we didn't get inflation under control, we were going to "have a big depression." He was instantly summoned to the White House and chastised for his candor. He was told he must never again use "the D-word."

This gentleman, who had a sense of humor, agreed. The next time he held a press conference, he warned that if we didn't get inflation under control, we were going to have "a big banana—a banana worse than the Great Banana of the 1930s."

I bring this up because I want to write about a word that I hear all too often at ConVal. Let's call it "banana."

I hear the B-word two or three dozen times a day at school. It is used as a noun, a verb, a modifier, or, most often, as an emotional intensifier: "I am banana tired of this banana banana, so don't banana with me, banana!" I hear it from freshmen and seniors, vocational students and college prep. I hear it from boys and girls about equally. I hear it in the halls, in the cafeteria, in the parking lot, in the gym, in the theater—anywhere students gather to socialize with each other. I even hear it in the classroom, but rarely addressed to me: if a student says "banana" (or "kiwi" or "mango" or "uglifruit") to a teacher, he or she gets sent to the office.

My students would ask, what's wrong with profanity?

Well, it's embarrassing when guests are around. One teacher told me she was walking a parent from the main office to the front door, a distance of perhaps 50 feet, and they heard "banana" three times. It's also boring and unimaginative the way students use it. Invective can be an art form, and even profanity can be colorful and witty if it's not reduced to a monotonous repetition of one-syllable words. When Mark Twain's wife tried to embarrass him into stopping his swearing by ripping off a string of oaths in public herself, he commented: "She knows the words, but not the music."

Finally, and worst of all, it's infectious. When I started teaching, I found myself swearing far more often. I'm ashamed to say that I even used "banana" in class once. You become desensitized to it. Discourse is brutalized. The school begins to sound like a prison yard or a war zone.

Profanity is appropriate in prison yards and war zones. I require my Modern Literature students to read books like Tim O'Brien's *The Things They Carried*, the best novel yet written about the Vietnam war, and watch *Slam*, a movie about a young man whose gift for poetry literally saves his life in prison. Both works are filled with profanity—if they were not, they'd be phony and absurd. It's all in the context. As O'Brien writes, "Send guys to war and they come back talking dirty."

You don't have to go to war anymore. My students hear words like "banana" in popular music, in popular movies, on television. They hear them on playing fields, at their places of employment, on street corners. They hear them in their homes.

So what's to be done? Installing a dress code is simple compared to cleaning up the rotten fruit in the halls. A student can deny saying "banana" a lot more easily than she can deny exposing her navel. And we can't send them home to change their vocabularies. (5/9/02)

The Home Stretch

Four weeks of school left—we're in the home stretch. On a race course, the home stretch is the last few yards of the race, the place where you find out what a horse is made of. You can learn a lot about students, too, by the way they respond to the home stretch.

Most of them finish in the middle of the pack. They run a respectable race, but they're never a threat to win. They didn't train hard enough, or they don't have the right bloodlines, or the surface of the track didn't suit them. There are horses for courses. That same girl who was the star of my creative writing class was screaming obscenities at her math teacher last week.

Some of them give up. That happened to one of my students last week—or maybe it happened earlier, when he missed seven out of ten school days for mysterious reasons. He came back promising to make up the work. He'd take all four quizzes he'd missed on Friday, after he'd finished reading the book. But then he was absent again Thursday, and I had a bad feeling. When I saw him in school the next morning, I almost stopped him in the hall to remind him that he had those quizzes to make up. But I didn't. And sure enough, later that day, he cut my class, so now he can't make them up, and his average fell below 40 percent for the quarter. He was never one of the favorites, but it made me sad to see him quit.

The favorites often lead wire-to-wire. They break fast out of the gate, they run easily in the lead, and they finish strong. Like thoroughbreds, they usually have good bloodlines—their parents were champions, too. They were trained well as colts and fillies to run hard and stay in control. They come from well-financed stables with winning traditions.

There are exceptions to the rule. Bloodlines have to start somewhere. The legendary Seabiscuit didn't have classic looks or champion parents. All he had was a huge heart that made him one of the greatest come-from-behind runners in racing history.

Heart is difficult to measure. I've got another boy who's been trailing the field the whole semester. He's very bright, but he fails to hand in work. There's something wrong—he's off his feed. I don't think he'll fail; he's been gaining ground in the last couple of weeks, but it's too late for him to finish in the money.

Sometimes early speed kills. I've had students who looked like world-beaters in the first quarter mile, but they fade in the stretch, especially now, when the weather gets warm and the sun is still out after supper and summer seems so near you can taste it. They coast in, finishing a respectable fifth, but wise bettors stay away from them. No heart.

Then there are the closers, the ones who come thundering up in the final furlong. They start from way back in the pack, and the race seems over, but here they come, eating up the turf with impossibly long strides, making the leaders look like they're swimming in mud, flying, stretching their necks and heads toward the finish line. It's breathtaking. There's nothing more exciting than a long shot who pays off.

I saw that happen in my Freshman Honors English class last fall. A girl who'd looked lost all semester suddenly lit up, and here comes Seabiscuit! She's asking the best questions, acing the quizzes, writing the best essays. It seemed to start when we challenged each student to give a speech that contained lessons he or she had learned. Hers was simple: she realized that to succeed, she would have to work harder than she'd ever worked before.

Four weeks to go. We're in the home stretch. Here they come! (5/23/02)

[24]

We All Teach

When I compared some of my students to thoroughbred racehorses with good bloodlines, a friend was upset. She thought I was suggesting that only children from wealthy families do well in school. "It wasn't true for me," she said. "My father was a farmer!"

It wasn't true for me, either. My father was a car salesman, and he was good at it. He took care of his customers. He told them that if they ever broke down, they should call him at home, and he'd come and fix the car—he could fix anything—or give them his car to use. I can't remember how many times the phone would ring, sometimes after midnight, and Dad would go out to rescue someone.

Dad believed—correctly—that if he took care of his customers, they would keep coming back to him. Late in his career, he was hired to coach young salespeople, but he soon quit in frustration. "All they want to do is make a quick buck," he told me.

My dad grew up on a farm. He went into the service when he graduated from high school, got to Europe just after the fighting ended, and drove a truck for a USO canteen unit. When he came back, he drove a cab. That's how he met my mother. They got married right after Mom graduated from high school. She wasn't even 20.

It must have disappointed her parents, both of whom were college graduates. My grandfather was a newspaper editor. I idolized him. When I was in eighth grade and had to write a report on my future career, I said I would become an editor. Selling cars was not for me.

I guess the ugly truth is that I didn't respect my dad as much as I should have. I figured I had nothing in common with him. I was more my mother's son, from the intellectual side of the family. And it's probably my mother's genes that steered me into college, made me a magazine editor and now an English teacher. (She'd be horrified to think she was in any way responsible for this catastrophe.)

But lately I've begun to realize how much of my personality I owe to my father. I don't have his ability to fix things, but I have inherited his even temperament and optimism, his faith that serving people ultimately pays better than shaking them down.

I wasn't planning to write a Father's Day column. But thinking about Dad has led me back to where I started—the direct correlation of parental income and educational attainment to performance in school. It's true; all the studies confirm it.

But studies deal with large numbers. My parents were high school graduates with a modest income, but they taught me to do my best. We all teach children, even if we have none of our own. We teach them by the way we lead our lives. If we conduct ourselves with honor and decency, like my father, we inspire honor and decency in young people. If we go for the quick buck, if we ignore the midnight call for help in favor of our own comfort—well, they learn that lesson, too.

I've met students at ConVal whose parents could buy mine, but they can't buy success for kids who don't give a damn. (6/6/02)

A Month of Sundays

When I first became a teacher, I remember hearing Ruth Ring, one of my colleagues, describe August as a month of Sundays. I didn't understand what that meant until I'd had a few Sundays as a teacher. Then it made sense.

On Sunday, a teacher awakes with a mild sense of unease that grows as the day goes on until, by Sunday evening, it's a full-fledged case of dread. Sunday night often features "teacher dreams"—horrible fantasies of unpreparedness and exposure. The class is totally out of control, and the principal is standing in the doorway looking grim. All the parents are watching as you attempt to teach a lesson, naked. Your own parents are watching.

I remember one vividly realistic dream in which I discovered I had apparently lost a student. It was during finals, and here was this name on the class roll, a student I'd never seen or heard of. The nightmare lingered even after I woke up. I drove to school feeling like something was missing.

Not all teacher dreams are awful. Sometimes they're just funny. Jackie Kelley, one of my English Department colleagues, dreamed I had asked her and her husband to come to my Freshman English class to sing "The Iliad Song." It was all about Homer's epic, and it went to the tune of "Edelweiss" from *The Sound of Music*.

That's a perfect example because teacher dreams resemble the classic actor's nightmare. You are standing on stage in costume, the theater is full, and you don't know your lines. You don't even know what the play is.

That's what teaching is like, too. You stand in front of a room full of adolescents who are waiting for you to entertain them. Unlike a theater audience, many of them don't want to be there. Some are barely awake. Some are ill. All are distracted by fears and desires that are far more important to them than whatever is on today's lesson plan.

If you aren't prepared, it's like doing stand-up comedy in front of a hostile audience. You're lucky to escape alive. During my first year, when I knew nothing about teaching and lacked any tools except my wits, I finished every class shaking and drenched with sweat, exhilarated if things had gone well, exhausted when—as was more often the case—I had failed to connect.

Things are better now. I have some tools, I have some experience, and, most important, I have some confidence. But it's the month of Sundays, and the dreams are coming back. (8/1/02)

Love and Work

Sigmund Freud is supposed to have said something like this: I know what a man wants—love and work. But what does a woman want?

Well, duh, Sigmund. A woman also wants love and work.

This is a story I tell my students when we read *Their Eyes Were Watching God* by Zora Neale Hurston, a novel that explores the relationships between men and women. To illustrate the point, I divide the class into boys and girls and ask each group first to come up with the top ten things a woman wants. When each group has its list, I write them up on the board. Then I ask each group to make a list of the top ten things a man wants, and I write those lists up on the board, too.

This activity produces 40 items and a lot of giggling. Everybody likes to talk about the differences between men and women, especially adolescents, who are just wading into the swamp. Like Freud, everybody seems to agree on what men want, if not on specific rankings. There's considerable disparity between the two genders when it comes to what women want.

When the laughter dies down, I ask the students to look at the 40 items and find common ground—what do both men and women want? Usually, it boils down to two things: sex and money.

I'm not surprised that teenagers choose to use the word "sex" instead of "love." Sadly, any high school kid talking sincerely about love leaves himself or herself wide open to ridicule, at least in public.

What concerns me more is the substitution of "money" for "work." I've done this exercise with several different classes, and out of the hundreds of items on the various lists, no one has ever come up with anything like "an interesting job" or "a fulfilling career."

When I ask them about it, my students seem puzzled that anyone would consider work an end in itself, something that gives pleasure or pride. To them, work means a painful or boring task, something to be completed as quickly as possible in order to move on to the finer things in life. That seems to be how a lot of students view their schoolwork. Is that the fault of the students? Or of the work we give them to do?

I don't want to make too much of this unscientific survey. Maybe it's developmental, and my students will, in time, come to realize the dignity and satisfaction that meaningful work offers. But it worries me. (8/15/02)

The Gospel of Literature

Every now and then some critic suggests that if students were to study the Bible instead of modern works like Allen Ginsberg's poem "Howl," all would be well. It reminds me of something that happened in my Modern Literature class a couple of weeks ago. In an essay on Christ symbolism, one of my students, intending to use the word "crucifixion," actually wrote "crucifixation."

It gave me a laugh and a useful new word: according to some of my students, "crucifixation" is the English teacher's disease. "You see religious symbolism in everything!" they accuse.

Guilty. In 1999, when I was a brand-new teacher, my Freshman English class was reading *The House on Mango Street*, a book by Sandra Cisneros about a young Latina named Esperanza. One of the chapters is called "The Monkey Garden," and I mentioned that any time a garden comes up in a work of literature, a careful reader should consider whether it is an allusion to the Garden of Eden.

The response was 25 blank stares. I paused. "How many of you know what the Garden of Eden is?"

Five tentative hands went up. I tried again. "How many of you have heard of Adam and Eve?"

Three more hands went up. Upon closer questioning, I determined that two of those students thought "Adam and Eve" was a fruit drink.

"All right," I said. "I guess before we go any further with this book, I need to teach you a little about the Bible."

A dozen hands shot up, and the owner of one of them declared, "You can't teach us religion, Mr. Clark. It's against the law."

"I'm not teaching you religion," I told the young lawyer. "I'm teaching you about your cultural heritage." Then I went on to describe what happened to Adam and Eve in the Garden of Eden and how that related to the way Esperanza lost her innocence in the Monkey Garden.

I wasn't trying to convert anyone. I was preaching the Gospel of Literature. That little lesson was enormously useful to their understanding of *The House on Mango Street* and, later on, *Romeo and Juliet* (who first declared their fatal love in an orchard), and *Little Women* (whose idyllic childhood home was called Orchard House).

Since then, I have handed students copies of a passage from the New Testament in which Jesus calls on his disciples to be "fishers of men," so that they would recognize the allusion in Ken Kesey's novel *One Flew Over the Cuckoo's Nest.* I have pointed out Christ symbolism in Melville's *Billy Budd* and Steinbeck's *The Grapes of Wrath.* We've panned for Biblical nuggets in William Golding's *Lord of the Flies.* Once, grappling with the problem of why bad things happen to good people in Tim O'Brien's *The Things They Carried*, I talked about the Book of Job.

In fact, studying modern novels and poems is a good way to get young people interested in the Bible. It is the source of the mighty river of English literature. It has provided plots, characters, cadences, and profound moral questions to writers from Shakespeare to Allen Ginsberg.

Study the Bible? We can't avoid it. But beware of crucifixation. (10/10/02)

Sublimation

I got an interesting email from a reader last week. He took note of my reservations about standardized tests and asked me to suggest a better method of assuring competency in important subjects. He also expressed concern about students graduating from local high schools with deficient math and science skills and challenged me to ask my students to do the following four tasks:

1. Name the two commonly used scales of temperature measurement and the freezing point of water in each of them.
2. Name the boiling point of water in each.
3. Transform the number 10 as expressed in base ten to base two.
4. Describe the physical process of sublimation.

I tried it with 50 students, ranging from freshmen to seniors. More than 90 percent knew that the two scales were Fahrenheit and Centigrade (or Celsius)—the spelling was spotty. About 70 percent knew that the freezing points were 32 and 0 degrees, respectively. Only 30 percent knew that water boils at 100 degrees C, and just 28 percent named 212 degrees F, which looks like an argument for metric measurement. (On the other hand, one student expressed the answer in liters, so maybe not.)

My favorite answer came from a girl who said the boiling point of water is "when it bubbles," and the freezing point is "when you can walk on it."

Alas, hardly anyone could do the math transformation (10 base 10 = 01010 base 2), and very few knew anything about sublimation, which is the "change of a solid substance directly to a vapor without first passing through the liquid state," according to the *Columbia Encyclopedia*. I had to look it up.

I tried the same questions on a number of adults, with almost identical results. And yet, all of those adults were gainfully employed citizens who pay taxes, raise children, own homes, and serve their communities in a variety of ways. Apparently, it is possible to survive and even, perhaps, to prevail without knowing anything about base two or sublimation, just as my worried correspondent has apparently suffered no serious consequences from his highly original use of apostrophes.

So what have we learned, class? Not much, I'm afraid. Each of us could come up with a list of things we think a high school graduate ought to know (Base 2? Apostrophes?), and each list would be different. The best definition of education I ever heard came from a dean at my daughter's college, who said it was "knowing what to do when you don't know what to do."

When I didn't know what sublimation was, I looked it up. Maybe we should give standardized tests in the library. (11/07/02)

What I Don't Know

One of my colleagues at ConVal recently told me that some of her friends had asked her if I was all right. They thought they had sniffed something sour or disappointed in my recent columns. It reminded me of a story about the late Cary Grant. At one point, a magazine editor wanted to determine his exact age and sent the actor a telegram: HOW OLD CARY GRANT?

Grant wired back: OLD CARY GRANT FINE. HOW YOU?

Old Tim Clark fine. Really. In fact, I couldn't be better. I don't regret leaving *Yankee*. I'm enjoying my students, enjoying my fellow teachers, enjoying my new career. I could go on, but it would sound sappy.

Worse, it would sound arrogant. During my first year as a teacher, I learned to be wary of what I called in my journal "the sine wave." Entries filled with optimism and pride were invariably followed by entries that read like suicide notes. As I tell my Mythology students, excessive pride is always followed by horrific punishment.

Worst of all, it would sound complacent, like I've learned everything I need to learn about this infinitely challenging job, and I haven't.

I don't know, for example, what to do about high school students who can't spell. I can help a good writer to write better, but I don't know how to teach a poor writer to write well. I blush to admit that, in spite of 23 years as an editor, I don't know enough about grammar.

I'm hazy on the retirement system. I don't know which line of my paycheck tells me what I'm making. I don't know what books students ought to read or what skills they must have to make a living in the 21st century. If I wanted to build a website, I wouldn't know where to start. I still don't know how to use an overhead projector.

I don't know how to teach a class of mixed abilities so that the brightest aren't bored and the slowest aren't overwhelmed. I don't know why some students just don't care about succeeding, and I have no idea how to change their attitude. I don't know what to say to a student who tells me she didn't do her homework because she's sleeping in her car.

The great Danish physicist Niels Bohr was walking along a beach with one of his graduate students, who was gushing about how much his teacher knew. Bohr picked up a pebble, showed it to the student, and said, "This is what I know." Then he turned and flung it into the North Sea. "That," he said, pointing to the waves, "is what I don't know."

I have been teaching now for three and a half years, and what I know about it is a pebble. What I don't know is the North Sea.

But I'm fine. Really. (12/19/02)

Read Fast, Say No

One of the brightest students in the Freshman Honors English class Lisa Cochran and I co-teach is a boy I'll call Harvey. Harvey is a terrific writer. His essays are detailed, fluent, grammatically correct, and full of insight and humanity. It's a pleasure to read them.

But Harvey has flunked our last two essay tests—not because his writing was poor, but because they were timed tests, and he didn't finish either one. In the first, students had to write one-paragraph answers to four

questions about *A Separate Peace* in 80 minutes. Harvey wrote two. In the second, they had to answer four questions about *Lord of the Flies* in 80 minutes, and Harvey managed to complete three.

We feel uncomfortable about what happened to Harvey, but we also feel stuck. Students need to learn to organize their thoughts and get them down on paper quickly. Why? Because that's one of the things they're asked to do on the NHEIAPs, New Hampshire's statewide test given to third-, sixth-, and tenth-graders. Later on, they'll have to do it on the SATs as well.

Will they have to do it in college or on the job? Probably. We are a society obsessed with speed: fast food, fast news, fast Internet connections, pedal to the metal! And like many other aspects of our society, this often goes directly against what we're trying to teach our students. Do a thorough job, we tell them. Don't rush—think it out first. Read the instructions carefully. Go back and check your answers. Revise, revise, revise.

But we educators don't always practice what we preach. We race through lessons to "cover the material," we penalize late assignments, and we impose a killing pace on ourselves as well. I just finished reading *The*

Gatekeepers, an inside look at how Wesleyan University chooses its freshman class. The admissions officers, who must read thousands of applications in a matter of weeks and reject three-quarters of them, tell themselves, "Read fast, say no!" It reminded me of what I tell myself when I have to read, correct, and comment on 25 essays in a day or two—read fast and say little.

Speed is almost always the enemy of good writing and good thinking. I spent 26 years writing for radio, TV, and magazines— some of it on hourly deadlines—and it was painfully clear that the less time I had to write,

the less detailed, fluent, correct, and insightful the product turned out to be. But that's what our students have to do on the NHEIAPs, so tough luck, Harvey. Next time, don't write so well. (1/16/03)

The Disease of Teachers

I spent a lot of my February vacation vomiting. After successfully avoiding the upper-respiratory bug that laid waste to so many last month (thank you, flu shot!), I fell victim to the stomach reptile just about 48 hours after it bit my wife. So as Garrison Keillor would say, it was a quiet week in Lake Wobegon.

But once the worst of it was over, we agreed that it was better to be sick during vacation than during school. At least it gave us time to recover. Had school been in session, there's no doubt that each of us would have gone back to work too soon.

It seems to be a chronic disease of teachers. We get sick leave, of course—it's guaranteed in our contracts. But there's a severe shortage of substitutes. One of my colleagues told me that on two different occasions he has called the sub coordinator to ask for a sub, only to have the sub coordinator call him back to say no subs were available. "I came in sick the first time that happened," my friend said. "The second time, I told him, 'that's your problem, not mine.'"

If you get a sub, you have to provide him or her with lesson plans for the day. In theory, teachers could have generic sub plans (watch this video, do that worksheet) available at the main office. In practice, it doesn't happen. A class block is 84 minutes long—not enough time to watch a whole movie, too much time to spend on a worksheet. You don't know who your sub will be—will it be someone who has read the book you're working on? You need a lesson plan simple enough for this unknown person (often roused out of bed before dawn) to handle yet challenging enough to keep your students engaged and active—maybe even learning something. So, more often than not, you end up going to school anyway, where you spend the day coughing, sniffing, running to the bathroom, sharing your germs, and prolonging your misery.

It wasn't like this at my old job. If I was sick, I stayed home. Voice mail would answer my phone. Email could wait. Paperwork could pile up on my desk. I could read or edit stories at home, and if not, I could always call in and ask somebody else to do it.

That won't work in a school. You can't teach by remote control. Teenagers won't sit there quietly like the papers on your desk, waiting for you to return. And your colleagues, though sympathetic, have their own work to do.

Besides, they don't know your class—who needs a kind word, who needs a kick in the pants. Kids aren't widgets to be stamped out on an assembly line, each one an identical product. You feel like you're the only one who knows them well enough to make that day a true learning experience.

I don't know about other teachers, but I get possessive of my students. I worry about having somebody else trying to teach them. And the funny thing is, I don't know what worries me more—that she would do a terrible job, or that she would do a better job than I would. That is the real disease. (3/13/03)

Bad Days

When I was in high school, I used to visit my father at the Pontiac dealership where he was a salesman. He had a little glass-walled cubicle on the showroom floor, but you couldn't see into or out of it because the walls were covered with so many Salesman of the Month awards.

I thought it was tacky—a way of showing off. I was too young to realize that the awards were not there to impress customers. They were for my dad to look at on the bad days that every salesman has.

Teachers have a lot of bad days, especially new teachers. I remember a conversation I had my first year with Will Steele, another rookie. It was at the end of a particularly bad day for both of us. He asked me how many good days I had in an average week. I considered it, then said, "One." He said it was the same for him. We looked at each other and contemplated why anyone would want such a job.

My ratio has improved considerably since then—in fact, it has probably reversed. I have four good days in most weeks, and occasionally five. But now, ironically, one bad day can spoil a whole week.

Take last week—please. It was the final one for two of my classes, Creative Writing and Mythology. I had started Myth by giving a pretest—22 simple questions, such as "What is the significance of Mount Olympus?"—so I gave the class the same test again and compared the results.

You know how it is with statistics. You can spin them any way you wish.

Spun positively, the test showed that the average score had almost doubled. But the average score, after nine weeks of lectures, reading, worksheets, and group projects, was 13 out of 22—59 percent. One student got eight right—both times. When I told her I was disappointed in her, she told me the course wasn't challenging enough.

That's the kind of thing that keeps me awake at night. I go to work each day charged up, determined to pour myself into my classes. I leap around like a madman, babbling poetry, making bad jokes, trying to show 90 adolescents what an adult who loves language and literature looks and sounds like. I end most days exhausted but feeling like some of that passion must have rubbed off on my students. Then I do my homework. I read their essays and grade their tests and go to bed wondering if I am wasting their time and my life.

What brings me back are little unexpected moments of grace. Luckily, I also had one of those last week. I asked my Creative Writing students to write a letter to the students in my next class, offering them advice about taking this course. Most of them were positive. Two complained that I had ruined their style or substituted my own for it—a charge I've heard before, when I was an editor at *Yankee*.

The most memorable one took a third path. "The most important things you'll learn won't be from Mr. Clark," she wrote. "They'll be from the crazy kid sitting next to you. This person will be the one you'll soon confide in.

He'll be the one who walks you step by step through anything. He'll be the one to tell it like it is, and for the next nine weeks or so, he'll be your teacher. So I hope you come to this class not knowing anyone, so you don't just sit with old friends. The unexpected doesn't come from the expected."

I'm going to put that letter up on the wall of my cubicle to look at on bad days. (4/1/03)

Blindfolds

There's a game I play with all my classes on our first day together. Half the class puts on blindfolds—we'll call them the students—and I give the other half—the teachers—a simple task to teach the students to do: have them stand in a circle facing outward, for example. Here's the hard part: the teachers are not allowed to talk to the students.

It takes a while for the students to realize that they will have to do all the talking—they can't just wait to be told what to do. Usually, they tell the teachers to clap hands once for "yes," twice for "no." Then, as in the game Twenty Questions, the students ask the teachers a series of questions to determine the nature of the task.

It seems impossible at first, and it may take 20 minutes to get the students to stand in that circle. But they are learning all the time. They learn, for example, that only one student can ask the questions, and only one teacher can clap hands. When more than one asks or answers, there's chaos.

After they try it a few times, switching sides to get a better perspective, the results are amazing. I had one group of teachers who got the students to lie down in a circle on their backs, heads in the center, and bicycle-pedal their legs in the air while singing "Row, Row, Row Your Boat." It took them five minutes. When I asked that particular group what they learned from the game, one girl said, "I learned we can do anything!"

The game is a powerful metaphor for what happens in schools. Being a student is like wearing a blindfold. It makes you feel nervous and vulnerable. You worry that people are going to laugh at you or play tricks on you. You instinctively get more cautious about speaking up. It makes you feel stupid.

It's easy for adults to forget how stupid we all felt in high school. As teachers, we are tempted to solve that problem by telling students what they need to know, or what we think they need to know. And that works, sort of. Some students dutifully write down what we say, study it, and repeat it on the quiz. Depending on how well they do this, we call them A, B, C, or D students. The others, who can't or won't, are labeled failures.

But in the game I play with my classes, the teachers aren't allowed to tell the students what to do. The students have to take responsibility for learning, and the only method is by asking questions. So the first lesson they learn is how to ask a good question. They soon realize that some questions can't be answered with yes or no. You need a third signal, which means "you're getting closer—ask it a different way."

It doesn't always work. If the task is too complicated, the students may get tired and bored. If the answers are too often "no," they go silent or rip off their blindfolds and quit. The teachers get frustrated, too—What's the matter with these dummies? In that sense, too, the game is like what happens in schools. Too many students, frustrated by a system that just keeps saying no, give in to apathy or rage. Too many teachers leave the profession.

But in the game, more often than not, somebody figures it out. Somebody asks the right question the right way, and bingo! The students are all down on the floor, legs pumping, singing "Row, Row, Row Your Boat," the teachers are laughing and cheering, and everybody feels like there's nothing they can't do.

If only every day in class could be like that. (4/24/03)

Bartleby in High School

Here's how naive I was when I became a high school English teacher: I thought my biggest problem would be that I wasn't familiar enough with 19th-century American writers. So after I left *Yankee* that summer, I read Melville.

As it turned out, my ignorance of Melville was the least of my problems. Ranking well ahead of that was my arrogance, my lack of teaching tools, and my lack of experience with emotionally damaged adolescents. At *Yankee*, I had worked with talented and industrious adults who loved their jobs. At school for the first time, I faced young people who didn't seem to care about anything. They didn't care about getting good grades. They didn't care if they didn't graduate. Their lives in school were a turbulent mixture of apathy and rage, and they could go from one to the other in an instant.

Some were bullies, thugs, deliberate saboteurs. Confronting them was terrifying, leaving me with shaking hands. The only way I could deal with them was to get them out of my classroom. But where were they supposed to go? They were not old enough to drop out, and the law guarantees them an education. So they sat in study hall (a great example of oxymoron) or in detention, or they wandered the halls. Often they just didn't bother to come to school. And when I marked them absent, I breathed a sigh of relief.

Others, however, were silent. They didn't cause as much trouble, but they didn't do any work, either. They were immune to threats, immune to sympathy, immune to offers of extra help. They slept in class or simply stared at the walls. They didn't frighten and anger me, the way the thugs did. They just broke my heart.

And I recognized them right away. I had read about them in Melville.

Melville's story "Bartleby the Scrivener" is about a man whose job was to copy legal papers—a human Xerox machine. It was brutally dull work, and the narrator of the story, a lawyer, is willing to put up with Bartleby's oddities—he eats and sleeps in the office, for example—in order to fill the position.

After a while, though, Bartleby begins refusing to do certain jobs. "I should prefer not to," he tells his boss politely, and no amount of threatening, coddling, or pleading will move him. In time, he does nothing but stare at a blank wall. The narrator— a kindly person, as shy of confrontation as I was when I started teaching—eventually moves his business to another building, leaving Bartleby behind like a piece of furniture. The next tenant, a practical man, calls the cops. Bartleby ends up in a debtor's prison, where his apathy is so profound he refuses food and wastes away, staring at the prison walls.

There aren't many Bartlebys at ConVal, but one or two are enough to suck all the energy, vitality, and community out of a classroom. Like Bartleby's employer, we teachers coddle, threaten, and plead with them, but to no avail. Somehow, their experience of the world has led them to the conclusion that the only power they have is the power to say no. And make no mistake about it— that is an awesome power. As the song goes, "Freedom's just another word for nothing left to lose."

It may be hard for the rest of us to understand that because we are industrious or talented or lucky. But if one feels sufficiently powerless, responding to the world with "I should prefer not to"— or its modern four-letter equivalent—makes a kind of sense. Unfortunately, it leads to starvation. (5/22/03)

What Should Students Read?

When I interviewed for this job, one of the first questions the committee asked me was this: What books should students read?

It's an obvious question, but I wasn't sure how to answer it. I'm still not sure. And the district isn't sure, either. A couple of weeks ago, all the middle and high school language teachers got together to discuss the new language curriculum, and most of the debate was about what books students ought to read.

Represented were two philosophical points of view, which I am about to grossly oversimplify. One was that our goal should be to teach students to love reading. Therefore, they should read whatever they enjoy the most, including what English teachers call "genre literature"—mysteries, science fiction, fantasy, Stephen King (he's a genre all by himself).

The other was that students need certain tools to learn how to truly comprehend what they read. "For the most part, kids today have no critical skills," one middle school teacher said. "They understand the words, but they don't get the subtleties—the theme, the tone, the style. They get the plot, but that's all." In order to teach the subtleties, a book must have subtleties. That rules out most genre literature; it requires classics like *The Odyssey*, *To Kill a Mockingbird*, and *Romeo and Juliet*.

But when we require students to read a book they don't enjoy and can't comprehend, the other side objected, we destroy their motivation to read: "They just say, 'This is stupid, I hate it, I don't get it!'"

True enough, the classicists replied—but if we never challenge students to read demanding literature, they will spend the rest of their lives skimming along the surface of things and never experience the joy of diving underneath to discover what treasures may be strewn along the seabed.

We didn't come up with any definitive answers, and that's what being a teacher is mostly about. When I started this column, my goal was to describe a teacher's life. I have learned that it involves many complicated problems to which there are no simple, obvious solutions. Every plan has something to recommend it, and every plan has drawbacks and tradeoffs. We don't generally get the luxury of choosing between right and wrong answers.

The great Danish physicist Niels Bohr (my unfailing source of provocative quotations) said there are two kinds of truth: trivial and profound. The opposite of a trivial truth is a falsehood. The opposite of a profound truth is a different profound truth. It is there, teetering on the fulcrum between warring truths, that a teacher lives. (6/5/03)

Graduation Day

ConVal's class of 2003 graduated last Saturday, and among them were 15 survivors of the first Freshman English class I taught in the fall of 1999, the class that nearly ended my teaching career after one week. Naively, I had told them I was new to the job and they'd have to help me. They reacted to this confession the way a pack of wolves reacts to the sight of a wounded caribou.

The most satisfying moment of last week's ceremony was seeing a member of that class receive his diploma. Six weeks ago, when it looked like he would fail my Writing About Music course and be unable to graduate, I mentioned him in this column. "Whatever I may have learned or however I may have improved as a teacher in the last four years," I wrote, "it hasn't been enough to help Simon." The irony is that, in the end, it wasn't me who helped him pass the course and graduate with his class. It was another student who unlocked Simon—or perhaps he only waited patiently while Simon unlocked himself.

The other student, whose name is not really Luke, was a friend of Simon's. Both of them had shaved heads, wore all-black outfits, and did not hide their disdain for society and its groveling minions. Luke and I clashed from day one, and I can't say I like him any better now than I did then. But he wrote brilliant, angry poems, and rarely have poets been model citizens. In the first few weeks, he did all the work required for an A+ with contemptuous ease. Then he devoted himself to driving me and the rest of the class to distraction.

In desperation, unable to control Luke's behavior, I asked him if he would tutor Simon. I think it surprised him. He thought it over for a moment, then asked if he could take Simon out of our classroom and work with him somewhere else. "There's no inspiration in that room," he sneered. I accepted that, with the proviso that he let me know where they would be. He agreed, and with that, the experiment began.

Nothing wonderful happened right away. Peter Nott, an aide who minds the Humanities Resource Center for the English

[49]

Department, asked me if it was true I'd given Luke and Simon permission to sit out there during my class. I admitted it. "They don't appear to be doing anything," he said. I asked him for his patience and said I would withdraw the privilege if they misbehaved. A day or so later, a shouting match erupted in the HRC between Luke, Simon, and a third member of my class. The upshot of that was that Luke's tutorial moved to the ConVal Corner Store.

By now, I was getting pretty nervous. I hadn't sought permission from anyone in the main office to untether these two menacing wordsmiths, and I still hadn't seen any writing out of Simon. So one day, I went down to the store, determined to pull the plug. When I got there, Luke was taking his ease in a recliner, and Simon was writing furiously. I turned around and tiptoed out.

Simon wrote eight poems, the minimum required to pass the course. They were depressingly similar, howls of pain filled with rage and obscenities, but they were poems. He showed me drafts and made changes when I asked for them. And on the day they were due, 40 minutes before the deadline, he sauntered into the classroom and dropped them on my desk, neatly typed.

Last Saturday, when the Class of 2003 processed into the gymnasium two by two, Simon and Luke marched side by side. I don't know if what I did was right, but I know I wouldn't have had the nerve to do it four years ago. So I guess it was a kind of graduation day for me, too. (6/19/03)

Be Every Day a Wirgin

When I was in college, I did a lot of acting. Once, a visiting director from Poland came to lead an acting workshop. What I remember best about it was his instruction: "Be every day a virgin." Because of his accent, it came out sounding like "Be every day a wirgin."

It was good advice, and it had nothing to do with sex. He was trying to get us to deliver each line as if we had never said it before, to hear every other actor's line as if for the first time, to be, as actors say, "in the moment."

It is hard to do. If you're like me, you are so worried about getting the lines and movements right, you stop listening to the other actors entirely. To an inexperienced (or bad) actor, a play sounds like this: "Blah blah blah my line blah blah my line blah blah blah my line."

This summer I learned a powerful lesson in acting from the magnificent James Whitmore, who played Grandpa in the Peterborough Players production of *You Can't Take It With You*. Jim is 82 years old. He first worked at the Players 56 years ago. In that summer of 1947, the founder of the Players, Edith Bond Stearns, bought him a bus ticket to New York so that he could audition for a part in a Broadway show, then gave him another night off to return for callbacks. He got the part and went on to win a Tony, which led to his distinguished career in films and TV, and which is why he comes back every now and then to do a show here. He's a classy guy.

I had a close-up view of 18 of Jim's performances, and not one of them was exactly like another. He varied his pace, his rhythm, his inflections. He stuttered, he coughed, he snorted, he broke into unexpected chuckles. He repeated some words and left others out. Sometimes he delivered his big third-act speech in a gentle, ruminative way; other nights it was furious and indignant. Somewhere in the middle of the run he broke into a little jig at one point, and in the last week, he threw in a ballet move.

We never knew what to expect. It was what I imagine playing jazz must be like.

And God help you if you didn't pay attention! If Jim thought your focus was wandering, he'd snap his fingers or clap his hands and demand that you look him in the eye—in character, in front of a live audience.

It was exhilarating, inspiring, and, to a person who doesn't make a living as an actor, terrifying. I thought the only way I could keep up with the professionals was to memorize each line and movement and never deviate from them. But Whitmore wouldn't let me. I found myself, perhaps for the first time ever, truly listening to another actor. And—not right away, but in time—I was in the moment. At the last performance, Jim suddenly turned and looked at me at a point where he'd never done that before. We both burst out laughing—in character, in front of a live audience.

So what does this have to do with teaching? Everything. A classroom is a theater with an audience of adolescents. It's essential to know your lines, but you have to vary your pace, your rhythm, your inflections. You have to talk about *Romeo and Juliet* or the Pythagorean theorem as if you had just discovered them. You have to really listen to your students, and if they stop listening to you, you may have to snap your fingers or break into a jig to get their attention. Otherwise, it's just blah blah blah.

You have to be every day a wirgin.

(8/28/03)

The Gorgon's Eyes

When I teach Mythology, I tell my students that these stories, though they may be thousands of years old, contain truths that can illuminate our lives today. There was a perfect illustration of it last Friday—and in Myth class, too.

One of my students—call him Rick—was having a bad day in a bad week in what's become a very bad school year for him. As the bell that signifies the beginning of class rang and the latecomers shuffled in—14 that day, a new record—I heard a burst of cursing in one corner of the room.

I hustled back to find Rick in a staring contest with another young man, whom I'll call Edgar. Edgar has problems of his own, not unlike Rick's. A girl was involved, too—she was the one swearing. I asked all three to sit down and focus on the class for a change.

As it happened, the students were presenting original myths that had to include all the elements of the Hero Cycle: the obscure birth, the tests and helpers, the journey to a dark place, and the eventual return to normal life. In many Greek hero myths, the hero and the monster he slays have something in common. When the hero kills the monster, he is symbolically slaying one of his own human failings—his lack of self-control, his greed, or, in the case of Perseus, his vanity. Perseus had to look in a mirror in order to kill the Gorgon Medusa, whose gaze could turn men to stone. The monster he saw in the mirror was the worst part of himself.

Things were going along fine until I heard muffled whispering from Rick and Edgar that quickly increased in volume and intensity. I went back again. "What's going on?" I asked.

"He's looking at me," hissed Rick.

"Tell him to stop looking at me," snarled Edgar.

I suggested that Rick go out of the room for a few minutes to settle himself. He left, muttering under his breath. I asked Edgar to calm down, too, and listen to the presentations. He leaned his head back against the wall and closed his eyes.

Things quieted down for a while, and after 15 minutes or so, I slipped out of the room during a presentation to retrieve Rick. He went back to his desk. Within a minute, the whispering began again.

This time I moved Edgar to a desk in a different corner, at the front of the room, and tried to turn my attention back to the projects. But it wasn't long before I noticed that Rick was staring fixedly into Edgar's corner. I turned around and saw the same hostile glare on Edgar's face.

I turned back to Rick and said, "Don't make eye contact with him."

"Make him stop looking at me," he replied.

Who was the hero? Who was the monster? I didn't know what they were angry about. Adolescent males can go to battle stations in an instant over a girl, a shove, a word, a look. Though Rick and Edgar have difficulty in school, they are both basically nice guys. I just wanted them to come back from whatever dark place they had gone.

I could feel the rest of the class watching. Measuring the distance and angles, I moved to a position directly between the two boys, so that neither could see the other. I hoped that would break the spell, and it did. We got through the rest of the class without incident.

But I won't forget their faces—like stone masks. They had looked into the Gorgon's eyes and seen themselves. (10/9/03)

Crossing the Line

Last summer I was working on a book about my first year as a teacher, and I told the story of how my favorite high school teacher, Mr. Teunis, drowned trying to save a student, one of several who were visiting him at his weekend place on the Shenandoah River.

I was shocked to hear of his death. Today, 23 years later, we would be shocked to hear that a single male teacher was entertaining a mixed group of high school students at a cabin many miles from the school and their homes. In fairness, I don't know whether there were parents or other adults present. It was 1970, so I suspect there weren't. I further suspect that nobody much cared about it.

Nowadays, teachers are routinely warned never to be alone in a classroom, much less a cabin, with a student, regardless of gender. Nowadays, teachers are reprimanded, and even fired, for "crossing the line"—getting too personally involved with students.

But the line is fuzzy. How close is too close? So much depends on the circumstances. Is it appropriate, for example, for a teacher to offer a student a ride home from school? Suppose the student is hitchhiking in the rain?

How about lending a student a dollar to buy a snack? How about five dollars for dinner? Should a teacher allow students to use his or her first name in the classroom? How about after school? Should a teacher hug a student? Should a teacher allow a student to hug her or him?

Last summer, my wife and I took in a student whose parents were working away from home in two different states. We've known her parents for years, it solved a problem for them, and it was no problem for us. She lived at our house for a few weeks. Was that inappropriate? The question never occurred to me. It does now, and it's chilling.

We've all heard horror stories about teachers, male and female, getting involved sexually with their students. That's clearly wrong, and those teachers deserve to lose their jobs.

We've also heard about teachers being unjustly accused by troubled or malicious students. A friend of mine who teaches college weathered such an accusation, fought back, and eventually his accuser admitted she was lying. But the damage had been done. He will carry the shadow of that accusation forever.

But it's not just jobs and reputations that are lost. What's also threatened by this growing atmosphere of fear and distrust is just the kind of relationship that made Mr. Teunis so important to my life. I never visited his cabin, but I spent hours in his office alone with him, talking about books, movies, politics, college—all the stuff I needed to talk about with an adult who wasn't my parent. It was in that office, as much as in the classroom or on the stage where he directed me in plays, that Mr. Teunis taught me how big and complex and scary and astonishing a world I lived in, and how reading Shakespeare and Hemingway and J. D. Salinger could help me love its beauty and endure its cruelty.

I didn't become a teacher so I could have the summers off to write books. I became a teacher to give that same gift to my students. I think most of us became teachers for that reason. Take it away, and what's left? (12/24/03)

My First Death

I often have trouble remembering names, a serious shortcoming for a teacher. Kids pass me in the hall, say "Hi, Mr. Clark!" and are gone long before my rusty retrieval systems can bring up a name. Oddly, though, the first thing that flashes into my head when one of those familiar but nameless faces goes by is something he or she wrote for me. "Cowboy boots," I think every time one girl goes by, recalling a poem she wrote about coming here from Texas.

So when I read of Rachel Perry's death from meningitis last month, my first thought was of a nameless poem she wrote in my Creative Writing class last year. Ironically, it was about a funeral:

> You looked different.
> It wasn't you who lay there.
> I stood there watching you:
> Your skin was yellow.
> Your hair was nicely combed.
> I was scared. The line was getting longer but
> I wasn't ready to move on.

Rachel is the first of my students to die, a sad milepost. There will be others. Joan O'Donnell, who retired last year, told me Rachel was the 32nd student she's outlived since 1980. "There were times when I was just relieved to get through a school year without anyone dying," she said.

I didn't know Rachel well. She was a quiet girl who wrote quiet poems. She graduated from ConVal last year and, according to her family, was saving money to go to college. She liked shopping and decorating and hardcore music. She pictured herself working with children.

One of the most heart-wrenching things about the death of young people is the briefness of their obituaries—no career highlights, no bowling leagues, no marriages, no children or grandchildren—nothing but dreams. They haven't had time for anything else.

A couple of weeks ago, just before vacation, I asked the students in my Modern Literature class to create maps of their lives, from birth to death. It's an assignment related to Kurt Vonnegut's novel *Slaughterhouse-Five*, in which a man learns from alien kidnappers to see all of his life as a single picture, a mountain range of joys and griefs, triumphs and disasters. Time is irrelevant and death is just one moment out of millions, each one existing forever.

It's a project most kids love to do, once they get over the initial creepiness of forecasting the moment and method of their own demise. They make up elaborate fantasies of wealth and fame: they marry movie stars, they become movie stars! One girl, whose past has been grim, got so excited about her future that she had to add paper to the top of her map to make room for her ecstatic visions.

Teachers have fantasies, too. "I touch the future," the bumper sticker reads. "I teach." When Rachel's future was lost, so was a part of my own, in which she writes glorious poetry, wins Pulitzers, and perhaps teaches other young people how to make their dreams come true.

Any pain I feel at the death of Rachel Perry is nothing compared to that of her family and friends, of course. But it is real. (1/8/04)

The Class From Heaven

Every teacher has stories about the Class From Hell. Mine was my first Freshman English class. When they were seniors, a couple of them admitted that they had tried to drive me out of the teaching profession. They nearly succeeded.

This is a story about the Class From Heaven: Modern Literature 012, whose final project I read and graded last weekend. But let's begin at the beginning.

It all started with a puzzle, a 1,000-piece jigsaw called Famous American Authors. In a way, every class starts with a puzzle—a collection of students who come from different backgrounds, with different fears and longings. They have to learn how to fit together. Some succeed, some fail. All of them take risks, and all of them learn something new about themselves before the class is over.

I gave this group the puzzle pieces, but I wouldn't let them look at the picture on the box. I said, "Your task is to put this puzzle together. The only requirement is that every member of the class take part. How you do it is up to you. Good luck."

Then I waited to see who would step up and take charge. Sometimes nobody does. In this case, though, I was confident. Freight Train was in the class.

Freight Train is the nickname I gave this particular girl back in her freshman year. She was in my Mythology class, which was made up of students from all four grades. She may have been the only freshman. In any case, I began that class by challenging them to recreate the Greek creation myth in four days, from Chaos to Pandora's Box. When I announced it, there was stunned silence. Then Freight Train got up and said, "Here's how we'll do it."

She didn't disappoint me this time, either. Within minutes she had the class organized—one group looking for edge pieces, another separating by colors. For the rest of the block, there was a nice, quiet buzz of conversation, with occasional bursts of laughter.

It took them three days to complete the puzzle. Every now and then I would say "Freeze." Then I'd ask them to tell me what they saw—who was in which group, who had taken some pieces off into a corner to work with on their own. On the last day, as the final pieces were about to be fit in, I called another freeze.

"I want everyone who is bent over the table right now to walk away from it and sit down," I said. Those people, our most passionate and obsessive puzzlemakers, looked disappointed, but they obeyed.

"Now everyone else move up to the table and finish the puzzle," I said. And the folks on the fringes, who had been elbowed out of the process, plunged in.

"You know what, Mr. Clark?" Freight Train whispered from the sideline. "It's kind of a relief to let somebody else finish." That's when I knew I had something special.

And it just got better. They did crazy skits about *One Flew Over the Cuckoo's Nest*. We dressed in black and held a funeral for all the characters who had died in the books, plays, and films we'd studied. Some of the eulogies were so eloquent they drew tears.

I threw college-level concepts like micronarratives at them, and they gobbled them up. We took a field trip to see August Wilson's *Fences*, then looked for connections to *Death of a Salesman*. They wrote poems about the soldiers in Tim O'Brien's Vietnam novel *The Things They Carried* and recited them to music. Freight Train wrote and sang an original song for it.

For the final project, I challenged them to write a modern novel. The only requirements were that it be at least 210 pages long, exhibit some or all of the characteristics of modern literature, and that every member of the class take part. There was shocked silence, then Freight Train got up and said, "Here's how we'll do it."

But this time, she wasn't the only leader. Others were stepping up, offering ideas about plot and characters. One girl volunteered to type and edit the whole thing. They spent the last three weeks of class working on it, a quiet buzz of conversation with occasional bursts of laughter: the sound of collaboration.

The novel is called *Blackjack*. It's 233 pages long. It's about a group of strangers who come together in a casino to play cards. They come from different backgrounds, with different fears and longings. Some succeed, some fail. All of them take risks, and all of them learn something new about themselves before the book is over.

I'm putting it in the ConVal library if you'd like to read it. It's by the Class From Heaven. (2/5/04)

Can't Do, Won't Do

I gave a test to my Mythology class last week. It was a mix of identifications, multiple-choice questions, short-answer questions, and analogies. I allowed students to consult their textbooks and notes, and to take the test home if they needed extra time. In short, it was a very easy test. It was designed so that nobody could possibly fail it.

Eight out of 25 students failed the test. How does one fail an open-book, open-notes, untimed, take-home test?

Three of them got low scores. They had problems reading the textbook, or they didn't take good notes. Some of them lost points because they spelled names wrong, even though they had the textbook in front of them. Call them the "can't do" students. They're trying, but they just don't get it.

The other five got zeroes on the test because they didn't even turn it in. When I asked them why, they said they forgot to do it. They said they left it at home. They said they were too busy. Or they just shrugged and said nothing at all. Call them the "won't-do" students.

As teachers, we have a wide variety of tools, resources, and strategies to help the can't-do students. We can tutor them after school or try alternative forms of assessment. We ask each other for tips, lesson plans, or projects or methods that have succeeded in similar situations. We call their parents and ask for help.

A lot of those parents are happy to cooperate. I had a student in last semester's Freshman English class who came after school every Thursday to get extra help because his father ordered him to do it. He never loved English, and he ended up with a C-, but he was one of my favorite students. It was a pleasure to stay late and help him because he was trying his best.

However, we have no idea what to do about the won't-do students. After-school tutoring doesn't help, because they don't ask for it and don't come if you offer it. Alternative forms of assessment, like hands-on projects, don't do much good, either. I've had my Myth class put out a yearbook for Mount Olympus High School, with gods and goddesses playing the roles of seniors. I've asked them to create movie treatments of love myths, updating the story to modern times and designing posters for their films. The five students who didn't bother to turn in their Mythology tests got lousy grades on those projects, too. It's the same story— minimal effort or no effort at all.

When I call the parents of these students, most of them promise to talk to their children about it. But I often hear resignation and despair: "I can't do anything with her," one parent told me. "He's 16," another said. "It's his responsibility to do his work, not mine."

I understand their resignation and despair, because sometimes I feel it, too. They're tired of slamming their heads into a brick wall of indifference. So am I. How easy it would be to stop asking why, to stop trying new ideas, to stop calling the parents. How easy it would be to just write the F on the top of the paper or test, record it in my grade book, and enter it on the progress report or report card. How easy it would be to go from can't-do to won't-do. (3/18/04)

A Joy and a Challenge

Two weeks ago, I wrote about the frustrations of dealing with "won't-do" students—those who have the intelligence and tools to do good work but, mysteriously, just won't. If all, or the majority, of my students were like that, I couldn't do this job.

Luckily, they aren't. So this week, I want to talk about the other end of the spectrum—those students who make a teacher's job a joy and also, perhaps, an even greater challenge.

There's a girl in my Creative Writing class who might be a great poet. I can't tell. I know she's a better poet than I am, and a better poet than any other student I've ever had in Creative Writing. I'm not a profound student of poetry, but I read it in the *New Yorker*, and this girl—let's call her Lily—writes at least as well as some of the poets I see published there. She's scary-good.

Here's a poem she wrote called "The Way It Happened":

> The sound her foot made
> Going through the wall,
> And the sound of her body landing
> After her horizontal fall.
> The way noise bleeds
> Through the drywall and the beams,
> The primer, the painted layers of sea green.
> The way the hole was not too wide
> To fix, and they layered more paint to hide
> The seams, the edges. The way
> The bruises faded, and were gone one day.
> The way the shallow ankle cuts
> Knit back together, the skin remade.

What am I supposed to teach Lily about writing? The best I can do is ask her questions about places I don't understand, or suggest that certain lines might be tighter, swifter, more exact. I'm not her teacher, but her editor. That's all she needs.

Then there's my whole Freshman Honors English class. It's not just that they're bright—I expect that from honors students. It's that they're so kind to each other, which is not always the case in such a group. Sometimes, it's the opposite.

Recently, we were reading the part of Homer's *Odyssey* where the Phaeacians honor Odysseus with a day of games. My co-teacher Lisa Cochran and I challenged our 39 freshmen to a series of our own games, all related to *The Odyssey*: storytelling, poetry, choral reading and dancing, and others. The last challenge was to string a bow, as Odysseus must do at the climax of the story.

We've done this particular challenge every year, and usually one or more students know the trick of stringing a bow and can do it in seconds. This year, we had nobody like that. So it turned into a problem-solving exercise.

They did it in teams, and everyone paid close attention. They tried different approaches, most of which failed, but nobody mocked anyone else's efforts. After 20 minutes, the last team managed to string the bow three times in three minutes, which made them the champs.

But the best part came after the competition ended. For the last five minutes of class, the people who had succeeded in stringing the bow taught those who hadn't how to do it. Everybody who wanted to try got another turn. And when the bell rang, one student said I should bring the bow back to class the next week, so that those who were absent that day could have a chance to learn it, too.

The joy of teaching such students is transcendent. The challenge is to be worthy of them. (4/1/04)

Dazzle Us

For several weeks now I have been pondering a remark in a letter to the editor of this newspaper. I don't recall the name of the correspondent, but she was critical of teachers in this district. She said something like this: Why don't the teachers dazzle us first, then ask for a pay raise?

I can't guarantee the accuracy of that quotation except for the word "dazzle," which has stayed with me. It's a powerful word. It goes far beyond "satisfy" or "impress" or even "astonish."

I'm not objecting to the word or the concept. I use a ten-point grading scale on oral presentations in my literature classes, and I tell my students that in order to earn a ten, they must "change the way I look at life." One of my friends urges his students to "be legendary!"

So yes, I want to be a dazzling teacher. But I have some serious questions about the task. Let me take them one at a time.

Dazzle whom? I assume the correspondent is talking about voters: "dazzle us," she said, in reference to the contract that was defeated by a handful of votes last March. But I suppose she could also mean students. Which students should I focus on dazzling? The high achievers? The low achievers? The vast indifferent middle? That which dazzles one student will baffle or bore another. And if by some miracle I succeed in dazzling most or all of them, how will the voters learn about it?

Dazzle how? How do I know a dazzling performance? Is it improvement in my students' grades? Scores on the NHEIAP tests? The SATs? If so, how big an improvement qualifies as dazzling? Beat the state and national averages? We already do that. Beat them by more? How much more? Or should I use my own definition of a dazzling performance in class—to change the way my students look at life? That's hard to quantify.

Dazzle when? One of the most satisfying parts of this crazy job is the moment when you see the light come on in a student's eyes. I'll never forget the day I read a poem by Robert Francis to a Modern Literature class. It's about how a baseball pitcher's aim is "not to, yet still, still to communicate/ Making the batter understand too late." At those last words one of my students, a pitcher on our baseball team who rarely spoke in class, whispered: "Perfect!"

He was, if only for that moment, dazzled. But that's rare. Like the batter in the poem, many students understand too late—after the test, after the class, after graduation, maybe after 20 years. "You plant these seeds," one of my colleagues was saying just last week. "You just lob them out there and hope that someday they take root." If we have to wait until all those seeds take root and flower, we'll never get a raise.

And finally, dazzle why? What's the real goal here? To get that raise? To be idolized by my students? "Dazzled" can also mean blinded or confused. In last week's issue of the *New Yorker*, Adam Gopnik writes about one of his favorite teachers and concludes that great teachers don't dazzle us: "The great oracles may enthrall, but the really great teachers demystify," he writes. "A guru gives us himself and then his system; a teacher gives us his subject, and then ourselves." (5/13/04)

Walking the Dog

"Write more about your wife," my agent said. She had just read the 60,000-word first draft of a book I spent much of last summer writing. At first, I had tried to interest her in a collection of these columns, but she quickly ruled that out. "Nobody publishes a collection of short pieces until the author is famous," she explained. So I wrote about my first year of teaching, that scary, depressing, humbling transition from veteran magazine editor to rookie educator at age 50. And she liked what she read. But she suggested adding more about my wife, who kept popping up in the book saying smart things and just generally being the most interesting character. So here goes.

I met May in college in the late winter of 1970. Her roommate was dating my roommate, but nothing happened between us until the following fall. I had Thanksgiving dinner at her mother's house in Connecticut, and it was that weekend, down on the rocks of Long Island Sound, that I first told her I loved her. She—so much wiser—replied with a two-syllable reference to bovine excrement.

Reader, I married her.

May has always had little tolerance for nonsense, which is exactly what my premature declaration of undying affection was. She knew I was getting ahead of myself, indulging in romantic dreams without thinking about the hard work required to make them real. I was still doing that in 1999 when I told her I wanted to leave *Yankee* and become a high school teacher.

By then she had already been working in education for 27 years as tutor, teacher, and school board member. "All right," she said. "But you don't know what you're getting into. Your first year, you won't be a good teacher—all you can do is survive. I'll do everything I can to help you, but you have to promise me you won't make any decisions about your future until after your second year."

As usual, she was right. I survived year one, leaning on her for help and support. I'm still leaning on her. Every day when we get home from our respective classrooms—she teaches sixth-grade

[67]

science and language arts in Jaffrey—we walk the dog and talk about our days. It is a 30-minute seminar in advanced educational philosophy and practice. I should claim it for professional development hours.

We exult in the lessons that worked and try to figure out what went wrong with the ones that flopped. She gives me advice about discipline and lesson plans. I give her ideas about writing prompts. The dog eats grass and occasionally stops to throw up.

We've always talked a blue streak, even when I worked at *Yankee*, but this is better. We have the same schedule now, the same vacations, the same passions and frustrations. We do our homework together in front of the fireplace on winter evenings. And in the middle of those awful sleepless anxiety-ridden Sunday nights, we assure each other that we're not bad teachers.

She makes less money than I do, which is obscene, but that's because superintendent Keith Burke was generous enough to credit me with 12 years of experience when I was hired. I won't turn it down. My experience as a magazine editor is worth an awful lot, but nowhere near as much as what I've learned while walking the dog with the smartest person I know. (5/27/04)

Mesa Verde

"What's missing?" Jim the ranger asked.

There were about 30 of us sitting or squatting on the sandstone shelf. We all looked at the ruins called Cliff Palace, and somebody said, "People."

"Too easy," the ranger said. "Try again."

"Wood?" a woman guessed.

"Okay," Jim said. "There's still some wood, but most of it is gone. What else is missing?"

I felt as stupid as my students must feel when I ask them the same question about a work of literature. "What's missing in this story? What's not there that ought to be there?"

"Some of the bricks are missing from the buildings," somebody guessed, and Jim nodded.

"Where did they go?" he asked.

"Were they destroyed by enemies?" another tourist asked.

"What enemies?" Jim replied. "When we look at this place, the first word that comes into our heads is 'castle.' We see fortifications, so we assume the people who built it must have done it for protection from enemies. But isn't a simpler explanation that the Anasazi might have simply torn buildings down and reused the bricks right here? When we look closely enough, we see signs of what you might call remodeling or redesign. Look at that tower over on the north side. What do you see that's different about it?"

And so it went, the ranger asking questions, the tourists trying to look at the familiar sight—all of us have seen the Mesa Verde ruins in postcards or books about the Southwest—with fresh eyes.

Jim explained that the archaeologists, too, had come to Cliff Palace with preconceptions. Then someone had the bright idea to ask local tribes, the Hopi, Navaho, and Pueblo people, what they thought of the ruins. "They taught us a different way of looking at them," Jim said.

The Hopi looked at three square holes in the uppermost level, and where whites saw windows, they saw the eyes and mouth of a kachina, a sacred figure who was looking down on and protecting the community. The Navaho also saw a kachina, but a different sort and in a different building, over on the north side. The Pueblo people were most interested in the arrangement of the kivas, round underground chambers. It looked to them like the people who lived in Cliff Palace may not have been related to each other, as the Western experts assumed. Maybe this was a way station, like the Far View Lodge we stayed in on top of the mesa, where migrants could spend a short time before moving on.

I knew a little about the controversy over what happened to the Anasazi, who built these amazing structures between 1200 and 1300 A.D., then disappeared. One school of thought holds that they were wiped out in war. Another says they were forced to move because of a 25-year drought.

"But there's no evidence of battle," Jim told us, "and they'd survived an even longer drought earlier. What we think now is that these dwellings were empty most of the year, except for people too old or sick to travel. In the spring, the men went out to hunt, going far into the mountains. Women and children farmed on the mesa top. They probably all came back in the winter because these south- and west-facing cliffs absorbed and stored heat, so they didn't need as much fuel to cook and keep warm. So the real question is not 'Why did they leave?' but 'Why didn't they come back?'"

I left Mesa Verde with my head spinning and my preconceptions in tatters. It occurred to me that learning is not always a matter of building up knowledge, brick by brick. Sometimes, it's about tearing it down and starting over. (7/22/04)

Getting Started

One of the problems I had when I started teaching was that I didn't know how to start teaching. What do you do on the first day?

I had plans, of course. I would have my students interview each other, using forms I made up with questions like "What's your favorite book?" We would all know each other better as a result, I thought. I was right—but not in the way I had expected.

My juniors and seniors in American Literature dutifully interviewed each other and dutifully reported what they had learned. That established the pattern for that class. They did what they were told, but without passion. Maybe the 7:30 start had something to do with it.

In my second class, a young man named James strolled in, looked around, grinned, and said, "I see we're all here!" James knew what I did not—that English on the Job might just as well have been called English for Students Who Hate English. It was like one of those German POW camps where they put all the escapers.

Clearly the interview exercise was unnecessary, so I junked it. I explained to them that we were going to approach English on the Job as if it were a job rather than a class.

"Excuse me, Mr. Clark?" James asked. "Does that mean we're going to get paid? And if we screw up, do we get fired?"

Everyone laughed. He had me, and they knew it. If they weren't paid and couldn't be fired, it wasn't a job. It was embarrassing, but I liked these misfits. They were full of life, and they wouldn't tolerate condescending nonsense.

The last class of the day was Freshman English. They did the interviews with minimal effort and a lot of whining and juvenile posturing. Half the class reported having no favorite book. It was depressing.

I went to see Gib West, the assistant principal, for some advice about the freshmen. "Take them outside tomorrow," he suggested.

"Tell them honestly how you felt about today."

It sounded good. So the next day I took the class into the fields and woods behind ConVal and tried to get a discussion of classroom behavior going. I was drowned out by the gripers. Clearly this wasn't working, either. So I told the students to walk back to the school without talking. Listen to the sounds of nature, I instructed, and we'll all write essays about what we heard.

Here's what I heard, marching at the end of the line:

"Why do we have to do this?"

"I'm hot."

"When does this class end?"

Then from the head of the column came a series of startled yelps, followed by screaming. I ran up and found a swarm of ground hornets clinging to the students' jeans and shirts, buzzing furiously. So much for the sounds of nature.

In all, five students had to be treated for stings. When the bell mercifully sounded, I went back to the English office, where the other teachers laughed and said I was already a legend. Then they told their own first-year horror stories to make me feel better. And I did, a little.

This week, we'll find different ways to get to know each other. I'll ask my Modern Literature students to put together a 1,000-piece puzzle without looking at the picture on the box, an exercise in problem-solving. The freshmen will play ball toss, and when somebody drops the ball, we'll learn how to talk about what happened and why without laying blame. In Creative Writing, I'll ask everyone to bring in an example of good writing and explain what they think is good about it.

But we'll stay out of the woods. (9/02/04)

Tell Stories

It's the season of writing college recommendation letters. I've lost track of how many students have asked me to do one. I always say yes—at first—but I also ask them to fill out a form available in the guidance office. It asks students to recall special experiences or lessons they remember from that teacher's courses, and it helps me tell a story about them. Stories are more powerful than adjectives.

Here's one I told about a boy in a Mythology class. They'd been assigned to research and make a visual presentation on an impossible quest. "Ron's quest was a World Series championship for the Boston Red Sox, and his visual was a piñata in the shape of Dan Duquette, the general manager who seemed the worst choice to achieve it. By the time all our frustrated Sox fans had finished bashing it with a Louisville Slugger, the classroom was powdered with pulverized peppermints."

You can also tell a story about a student's reaction to failure. Describing a group project organized by one student, I wrote: "It was a disaster. The slackers mumbled, the thugs grunted and belched, and the lamebrains read the wrong parts at the wrong times. Erin darted around, improvising transitions, adlibbing brilliant bits when she could, and smiling gallantly, but it was no good. I gave the group a D. Erin never whined about it. Erin's not a whiner."

You also need to consider your audience. Admissions officers read hundreds or thousands of teacher recommendations, all of them laudatory. Sometimes I try for a bracing splash of cold water. "Ian made an instant impression freshman year when he remarked that, while he didn't think I was a very good teacher, he was impressed by the fact that I knew nearly as much as he did. As Ian himself now acknowledges, 'When I was a freshman I was a proud little snot.'"

If there's nothing much to say about a student's performance in class, I look at other arenas, like sports. One girl played goalie on the lacrosse team: "Goalies have to have courage," I wrote, "the physical kind that can withstand hard rubber balls being fired at them from all angles and the moral kind that accepts the responsibility of being the last line of defense."

It's hard to write about quiet kids. That's where anecdotes are especially useful. "Amy volunteered to take all the individual squares her classmates made and sew them onto a piece of backing so that we could hang the quilt on the classroom wall. That's the sort of person Amy is: the plain background against which more colorful personalities can stand out, but without which the whole quilt would fall apart."

It's even harder to write about a kid I never figured out. For a mysterious boy who was in my Writing About Music class, I described his final project: "He and his partner wrote a hip-hop opera (or 'hip-hopera,' as they called it) that was received so enthusiastically by the rest of the class that I think I saw Nate smile. But I could be wrong."

Hardest of all is finding something positive to say about a student whose performance can charitably be described as indifferent. I usually tackle it head-on. "He is, in short, a fairly typical messed-up adolescent boy who is trying to get his life straightened out. Of course, this makes him a risky choice for your next class of students. But I think he's worth that risk. The same energy and intelligence that makes him an occasional pain in the neck in class could make him a standout in college and beyond. I hope you'll give him that chance."

This fall, for the first time, I told a student no. At first I said yes, though he once submitted an editorial to the school newspaper calling me a lousy teacher. That would be a great opening line if I had something wonderful to say afterward. But he hasn't shown me anything since then, and I can't tell a story about nothing. (10/28/04)

Good Intentions

I bought a cup of coffee at a ConVal soccer game recently, and the lady who sold it to me introduced herself as the mother of one of my former students. We chatted for a minute, and then, out of the blue, she said, "When I started reading your columns, I thought you didn't like students. But I asked my son, and he said it wasn't true."

I was stunned. I went back and reread every column I'd written, trying to see them through objective eyes. It was hopeless, of course. I couldn't see it.

That doesn't mean it isn't there. When I teach literature, I often have students tell me, "Oh, come on, Mr. Clark. You're reading way too much into it. The author didn't mean that." When I tell them that every word in a good book is carefully chosen, every symbol and metaphor intentional, they find it hard to believe. "If that were true," one of them argued, "it would take years to write a book!"

But the author's intention, while important, is not the exclusive source of meaning. Writers are people. They bring all their experience, all their upbringing, all their blind spots and prejudices to what they write. Good readers bring their own lives to books, too, and often find meaning in them that the authors probably never intended.

Once, in the Honors Freshman English class Lisa Cochran and I co-teach, we played a game that involved our students tossing three balls around a circle. It's a good community-building exercise that allows you to talk to students about teamwork and problem-solving.

In this game, however, we went a step further. We asked the students what else might this game be about. We had been studying symbolism, so the kids started thinking about the balls. One of them was black, one was white, and one was a fuzzy yellow tennis ball. They started to consider what the colors might stand for and how the fuzziness of the tennis ball might be interpreted.

They had an interesting conversation and came up with remarkable connections to the reading we'd been doing, to the real world, and to their own experiences.

When they were done, they asked us if they'd gotten the right answers. We shrugged and told them we didn't know. We hadn't had any special meaning in mind when we chose the balls.

"So it was fake?" they asked, feeling tricked.

Not at all, we told them. You created the meaning. You saw it, you explained it, you cited evidence for it. It exists, whether we intended it or not.

All writers understand that when you publish something, you lose control over it. People read it and come up with their own interpretations. Or history intervenes. A friend of mine wrote a song containing the line, "I forget that there's a sky over Manhattan until it does something." He told me many people asked him if it was about 9/11. He wrote it years before the event.

Looking back, I guess that what the lady who sold me the coffee was referring to were columns about students with problems—students who make life difficult for their teachers, their families, and most of all themselves. They're part of a teacher's life, and this column would be phony if it didn't include that part. It would also be phony if I didn't write about great students, which I've done many more times than I've written about troubled ones.

I have to write about students, good ones and otherwise. Good writing needs details. I'll change their names, but surely some of them will recognize themselves, and their feelings will be hurt. That's not my intention. But I know from years of marriage that when you hurt someone else's feelings, your intentions are meaningless. You have to deal with the hurt feelings.

I'm sorry if I offended anyone. (11/11/04)

Stories from the Cockpit

A long time ago, when I was still writing feature stories for *Yankee*, I interviewed a pilot for one of the major airlines. I forget how I found this guy, but he was willing to talk to me, so I visited his home in Connecticut. We sat at his kitchen table, and he started telling me stories—the kind of stories, as my editor said later, that pilots usually only tell other pilots.

He told me about two pilots who got into a fistfight in midflight. He recalled one pilot who was famous for consistently making too low an approach to a certain New England airport. It got so bad that other pilots with experience refused to fly with him. One day he approached the airport even lower than usual and flew his loaded airliner into the ocean.

The most amazing story of all was about an entire flight crew that fell asleep. The plane's destination was Los Angeles, but it was headed right out over the Pacific Ocean before frantic ground controllers found a way to trigger a fire alarm on the flight deck to wake the pilots. "They hushed it up," he added.

I wrote a dandy story and, as was my custom in those days, sent the pilot a copy before publishing it to make sure I had the facts right. He called me right back. "If you print that story, I'll lose my job," he said. I checked with my editor, and we decided not to print the story. Three years later, the story of the sleeping crew surfaced in the *New York Times*.

Sometimes I feel like that pilot. I could tell you some amazing stories, but if I did, I might lose my job. I'm only half a journalist. My other half is a teacher, who has legal and ethical limits on how much I can say about my students.

My two halves are constantly fighting with each other. I know a student whose story is so inspiring it would bring tears to your eyes. But if I told it as well as that student tells it, using details that make you taste and smell and feel the terror of abuse, a couple dozen people would instantly recognize the child. I don't think the student would mind, but that student is a minor. I'd have to seek the permission of the parent—who is not the abuser—and I don't see that happening.

Some writers in my situation have relied on composites—putting together parts of the stories of many people to create one—but that approach, while preserving the privacy of the students and their families, is a flat violation of journalistic ethics. A *Washington Post* reporter was stripped of a Pulitzer Prize for it.

Well, people ask me, why not just write about good students? Aren't the majority of students at ConVal smart and funny and kind and respectful? They are, and I do write about them. But every teacher knows that they are not the students who monopolize your time and attention. They are not the students who send you home at night wondering why you ever decided to be an educator. They are not the students teachers talk about only with other teachers.

Why, one teacher I know told me about a student who did something so outrageous that she—but I can't go on. Somebody might figure out who it is.

So I can't really tell you about all the everyday dramas that happen in this school. Maybe that's best. Maybe the passengers shouldn't know everything that goes on in the cockpit. (11/24/04)

You Never Know

Each student is a mystery. Many come with some kind of label attached—high achiever, sleepyhead, troublemaker, even, as one of my colleagues puts it, "oxygen thief." Mostly the labels are accurate, but you never know. Sometimes one comes along who turns the stereotype on its head.

I had a student like that in Creative Writing recently. His label said, disapprovingly, that all he wanted to write about was fire-fighting.

It was true. Jeff wrote about nothing but firefighting. He wrote a lengthy short story—almost a novella—about one particularly dangerous fire in which some firefighters are trapped in a burning house. It was filled with the kind of specific detail that tells a reader immediately that the author knows what he's talking about—the clothing, the equipment, the specialized language.

When I saw his first draft, I noticed he had crossed out some dialogue that contained profanity. "Is this how firefighters talk?" I asked him.

"Yes," he said.

"Put it back in," I said.

Late in the course, I suggested he try some poems about fire-fighting. He was dubious at first, but then produced a series of terse, exciting poems that capture the danger, excitement, and moral complexities of a firefighter's life. My favorite is called "I Wonder."

> The dispatch was unknown medical emergency.
> We get out of the rig. I can smell the dew on the grass.
> I can see the sun starting to poke above the horizon.
> I walk up to the door, clueless:
> Would this be a little girl, splinter in finger?
> Or a grown man, not breathing?
> Or a crazed heroin addict, waiting there
> With a 2x4, waiting for us to come through that door?
> Or would this call be that call

Where we go in, and the bullets ring out?
I reach my hand up for the doorbell,
Sweat running down my forehead:
The door flings open.

I read it to the class, and when it ended, there was a groan of disappointment. "What happens next?" they demanded.

The author just grinned. "You never know," he said.

That's what teaching is like, too. You get a class roster before each course begins. Some of the students listed on it you have had before, some are new. You ask other teachers about them. You count the IEPs, the Individualized Education Plans for special education kids. You try to avoid labeling, but sometimes you can't help it. "This will be a tough one," you think, or "I can't wait to get started!"

Then the door flings open. (12/9/04)

Vinaigrettes

We were sitting around the English office during prep block the other day, listening to our two newest and youngest members of the department giving each other grief. They do it for fun, and we enjoy it, too. I remarked that they reminded me of Tracy and Hepburn.

"Who are they?" Tracy asked.

It's bad enough when my freshmen don't recognize my cultural references. When other teachers are too young to get it, I feel prehistoric. So I explained about Kate Hepburn and Spencer Tracy, told some funny stories about them, and recommended that our battling newbies rent *Adam's Rib* or *Pat and Mike*.

Tracy was still stewing. "I don't know if I've been complimented or insulted," he said.

Complimented, I assured him, and went back to correcting.

A minute later, Tracy said, "You give great compliments. One compliment from you is worth ten from Mike here," gesturing at Mike O'Leary.

Without a moment's hesitation, Mike said, "That's pretty clever, coming from you."

Mike's comebacks are legendary, if occasionally unprintable. Here's one from earlier this year. Jeff McGlashan, our Most Voluble Player, was going on with great perspicacity about something or other when Mike looked up and said, wearily, "You don't have an 'off' button, do you? You're either 'on' or 'more on.'" Then his eyes widened. "Hey! 'On' or 'moron'! That's good!"

Jeff laughed as hard as the rest of us and went on talking.

Most of the time, we're laughing about things that happened in class. Kids say the darnedest things, as Art Linkletter (never mind) put it, and they write them, too. Just last week, one of my Journalism students referred to "cracked troops." In another classroom, I saw that students had written something about "pre-martial sex." Maybe that's why the troops were cracked.

The laughs in student work aren't always mistakes. Sometimes they just reflect the interior life of adolescents. I had a student in

Creative Writing who wrote a fine story about a young man who is captured by a vampire. The vampire not only drinks his blood, he trains him in vampire skills, including flying. When the boy's apprenticeship is over, the vampire turns him loose. The boy flies back to his own house, looks in the window, and discovers that (gasp!) his parents have moved his stuff! He righteously bites their necks for this terrible crime.

There is also a special category of spell-check errors. Among them, I have found a soldier who joins the "Green Barrettes," a thoughtful analysis of how Sandra Cisneros tells stories through "vinaigrettes," and (courtesy of team leader Jill Lawler), the tragic story of a student who wrote a long piece about the writer Virginia Woolf, in which spell-check changed her first name to an anatomical feature I'd prefer not to mention.

And sometimes, the mistake captures an elusive truth. I'm thinking of a student who explained an obscure reference "in lame man's terms."

I don't mean to suggest that all we do is sit around exchanging witticisms and laughing at students. But it's important that we like each other, that we tell jokes and goofy stories from the classroom. These little vinaigrettes add flavor to our days. (1/20/05)

Bomb Scare

The first semester at ConVal ended last week with a bang—literally. Somebody shattered a toilet bowl in the downstairs boys' bathroom with an explosive device, probably a firework of some kind. A couple of my Journalism students spotted the commotion and acted like journalists, which made me proud. They hung around, pestered administrators, custodians, and bystanders for quotes, then came racing into the classroom and started writing.

An hour later, a girl told the administration she'd found a bomb threat in the downstairs girls' bathroom. The administrators had no evidence the two events were linked, but the coincidence made them uncomfortable enough to order everyone at school to "shelter in place."

By then I was in the cafeteria on lunch duty with half a dozen other teachers. We herded the complaining multitudes into the theater and locked the doors. There were about 250 students and other teachers jammed in there (seating for 200), including a Theatre Arts class in full costume and makeup that was about to put on their final exam.

I added two and two and surmised it was not a drill. Then everything changed again. We were all told to leave the theater, get our outdoor clothes on, and move outside into the parking lot to our prearranged fire drill assembly points. It seemed odd at the time, but we later learned that a third suspicious event had just occurred, which I'm not going to describe for fear it will give somebody else ideas.

It wasn't as cold as it had been recently, but it was cold enough. One of my kids saw another student with a white face and asked me if she had frostbite. It was one of the theater students, still in makeup.

A number of students were missing and had to be run down or accounted for. While police and staff searched the building, rumors blossomed in students' minds. Cherry bombs mutated into real bombs, and an M-80 (a powerful firecracker) turned into an M-16 (an assault rifle). Students everywhere were on cell phones, and the office phone lines were jammed with anxious parents calling in.

After the gymnastics room had been searched, administrators gave the okay for lightly dressed students or those with medical conditions to go inside. But the word never got down to me or to many other teachers. When kids got into cars to warm up, we rousted them out, as has always been the custom. There aren't cars enough for everyone.

Then we got word to let them get into cars, but they were not to leave. Then, when the buses started arriving, we were told not to let students with cars leave until the buses had been loaded. Then that was countermanded, or so we thought, and the parking lot became a nightmare of cars weaving between crowds of students and teachers. It turned out there had been no such release order—some kids just made it up.

Eventually, everyone got home safely. It was a discouraging experience in many ways, and I found myself thinking about a day in the spring of 1971 when I watched Harvard's Center for International Affairs burn. Somebody had set off a real bomb in it to protest what they thought was its role in the Vietnam War. A young professor of mine stood next to me and said he felt like a blacksmith in 1920. He thought the university was finished.

But he was wrong. Universities aren't finished, and neither are public schools. Our cold, frightening, confusing, and depressing day was only that. Everyone came back the next day, and we started exams. (2/3/05)

What They Do

The bad boys sit in the back, of course, where it's hard to see them sleeping, or passing notes, or just generally raising hell. The goodie-goodies sit in the front row and raise their hands a lot. The silent majority sits in between, but not silently. Silence only happens when they're asked a question.

They always sit with their friends. This is an iron law. If you don't make them engage in community-building games and exercises, they will spend months together without learning anything about each other, not even each other's names. Besides, if they weren't with their friends, to whom would they talk when they shouldn't be talking?

Some drift in late and take seats as close to the door as possible. That way they're less likely to be spotted as tardy—plus they can get out in milliseconds when it's time to leave.

They eat, although they're not supposed to. They drink liquids other than water, although they're not supposed to. Often, the simplest instructions have to be repeated. Ask them to count off by fours, and somebody always says "five!"

There's not much in the way of meaningful discussion. Oh, the usual suspects will share their thoughts and feelings, often at length. This earns them rolled eyes and dirty looks from their neighbors, who want nothing more than for the pain to end as quickly as possible.

It's hard to blame them. They're not there by choice. Much of the time, they are forced to endure an hour or more of someone droning away about things they don't care about or understand. That's why, when asked if there are any questions, many of them ask questions that have already been answered. Then it's the guy at the front of the room who's rolling his eyes and giving them dirty looks.

Every expert in education, every field study, every psychological test tells us that the worst way to convey information is talking. I had a friend at *Yankee* who spent some time teaching school before becoming an editor (what a concept!), who used to laugh about it. "If the purpose of schooling is to teach students to communicate effectively," he'd say, "why is the teacher the only one who's talking?"

It's not always that way, of course. I'm indulging in some hyperbole—a literary term for exaggeration that is not intended to deceive. Sometimes there's genuine dialogue; sometimes I come out of the room excited and engaged and looking forward to the next time.

But there's enough truth in it to be unsettling, because it doesn't fit my expectations, my notion of what it is we're supposed to do when we are in this room together. When I first came to ConVal, I was shocked by it.

I'm not shocked anymore. Gradually, inevitably, I have grown accustomed to it. I make excuses for it—it's late in the day, everyone is tired. All of them—those doing the lecturing as well as those being lectured—have lives of their own and things to do they find more urgent, more interesting, more important. I've grown a thicker skin. I had to, or I would have quit long ago.

After all, we only have faculty meetings every other week. (3/31/05)

Recognition

We had a Recognition Assembly in the gym at the end of school last Friday. It was intended to honor students and teachers who have accomplished remarkable things this winter. As Lincoln said at Gettysburg, "It is altogether fitting and proper that we do this."

But I watched it this time from a unique perspective. And I recognized something that troubled me.

All 1,200-odd students were there. The school band was set up at the eastern end of the gym, playing a demanding orchestral piece called "Inchon," which commemorates a great battle of the Korean War. It starts very quietly, with the sound of waves on a beach and a flute solo, pianissimo.

Band Director David Aines waved his musicians off after a few bars. The students in the audience were making too much noise. While he pleaded for respectful attention, I climbed up near the top of the bleachers against the western wall, as far away as it was possible to get from the band. I knew what I would find up there. There were about a dozen students raising hell, talking in loud voices, giggling, eating snacks, jeering at the musicians, or conspicuously ignoring the performance. Or perhaps they were putting on a performance of their own.

Social studies teacher Nancy Gagnon was up there, too, but she was outnumbered. I joined her, and we tried shushing them. They got a little quieter, but they still weren't paying attention. They knew this assembly was not for them.

At first I was angry, but then I started to feel sad for them. It's hard enough to spend their days in a place where they consistently fail. To be forced to spend the last hour of another discouraging week celebrating those who succeed, to be forced to listen to accolades for students who have won academic, artistic, or sporting laurels, to have their noses rubbed in their own dim prospects is cruel indeed.

These sullen, disobedient oafs were all fresh, beautiful, bright children once, before the relentless culling process began. The

[87]

sorting-out may have started 10 years ago, when teachers put books in their hands, maybe for the first time. Or perhaps it was when they first stared blankly at a page of numbers and felt the panic rising inside. For all of them, there must have been a moment when they recognized that a world full of possibility had turned into a weary trudge up a long, long hill.

I didn't know any of them. My schedule is filled with honors and college-prep classes. Many of my students struggle with academics, but at least they still struggle. There wasn't much fight left in these kids, except the daily battle against humiliation.

I'm not naive. I know that next week I'll be losing my temper with these same kids or others like them. They are the ones who wander the halls aimlessly when they're supposed to be in class, who use foul language incessantly, who clog the halls during passing time and ignore polite requests to keep moving.

But this day, as the Recognition Assembly drew to a close, I found myself talking gently to the lost souls in the top corner of the bleachers instead of snarling at them. "It will only last a little longer," I whispered, the way one whispers to a child who is frightened or in pain. "Just a few minutes longer." (4/14/05)

Multitudes

I don't have much to say about the last two weeks at ConVal because I wasn't there. On the evening of May 11, I got the phone call all parents dread. Our son Joel, who was ten days away from graduating from Bard College, had fallen 30 feet out of a tree and broken his wrist and back.

Within hours May and I were on our way to Poughkeepsie, New York, where we spent the next ten days and nights. On the way, we reminded ourselves how lucky we were: Joel was alive, and he could move his arms and legs. Two years ago, when May's brother fell off a roof and survived, we learned that half the people who fall from 25 feet are killed.

Another stroke of luck was that the ambulance had bypassed a closer hospital to take Joel to St. Francis Hospital, a regional trauma center with a full complement of specialists, including a neurosurgeon, Dr. Krishna Murthy, who assured us the day we arrived that although Joel would need surgery on his back, if all went well he would be on his feet two days later and able to leave the hospital in five. Other doctors who cared for our son—there were almost a dozen eventually involved in his case—were more cautious, and some of the nurses actually rolled their eyes.

We spent the next four days waiting. The beauty of a trauma center is that when you arrive badly hurt, everyone drops everything to tend to you. The disadvantage is that once you're stabilized, you are the one dropped when the next trauma patient comes in. There were ten trauma cases in the next two days. Joel's surgery was put off twice. He was not allowed to wash—his hair was still full of twigs and dirt from the fall—nor even to raise his head. We ate and slept in his room, bringing cups of water to his lips when he was thirsty.

On Monday, he had two operations in succession—first on his spine, then on his shattered left wrist. He was under anesthesia for seven hours. When he awoke, he was still being moved from the OR to the recovery room. The pain was indescribable. He was on the maximum dosage of morphine, which he controlled himself

[89]

by pushing a button. Even so, he could only give himself more of the drug every six minutes. "Time him," a nurse advised, so for an hour we watched the second hand sweep by, telling him the instant he could push the button again.

On Wednesday, having been fitted for a brace, he sat up for the first time in a week. He was so dizzy that three of us—me, May, and Brenda, his physical therapist—had to hold him up. When his vertigo passed, he put his feet on the floor and, with all of us buttressing him, he stood up.

"Do you want to try a few steps?" Brenda asked.

"Yes," he said. He shuffled forward two steps and stopped. Then he backed up to the bed, and in slow motion, we lowered him and returned him to his back. All four of us were drenched with sweat.

That was the day Joel vowed to attend his graduation ceremony on Saturday. Again, eyes widened, and there were words of caution. Only Dr. Murthy nodded and said it could be done.

On Saturday afternoon, he graduated with honors. When his name was called, Joel's friend Max, who was with him when he fell and made the 911 call that brought the first responders, pushed his wheelchair across the platform. A few yards short of the podium, he stopped. Joel stood up and walked forward to accept his degree, unassisted.

I say "unassisted," but of course that's not true. Joel is brave and strong and resourceful, but at his elbow were multitudes: ambulance drivers, doctors, nurses, technicians, clergy, administrators, food service workers and cleaning staff from St. Francis; Bard's EMS team, professors, administrators, and students; teachers, students, and staff from ConVal and South Meadow School and the Dublin Consolidated School; and loving relatives and friends across the country. We owe them all our thanks. (5/26/05)

Triage

When my son Joel (he's feeling better, thanks) found out I'd written a column about his accident, he said, "What's that got to do with teaching?"

Nothing, I guess. I just couldn't think about anything else at the moment. But since then, I've been thinking about connections between schools and hospitals. We spent ten days eating, sleeping, and hanging out in one, getting to know the nurses, meeting other families in crisis, and just generally living in the belly of the beast that is modern medicine.

Hospitals, like high schools, are big, complex institutions with lots of rules. Otherwise, there'd be chaos. If you're lucky, as we were, you'll be in a critical care ward, where the nurses are experienced, smart, kind, and funny. They also know when to enforce a rule strictly and when to bend it a little to help a patient heal.

The downside is you have to be seriously injured or sick to be in critical care. After Joel's surgery, we moved upstairs to what they call "a medical floor," and the care got—not worse, but more impersonal. We were no longer in crisis, so we got less attention.

Patients use wildly different strategies to gain the attention of nurses and doctors. We spent a lot of time getting to know them personally, learning their names and greeting them warmly whenever we saw them. When we wanted something from them, we asked for it in as respectful a way as we could manage, and it usually worked.

Not all patients and family members are so diplomatic. The nurses told us about patients and their relatives who swore at them, whined, griped, and broke big, important rules, like no smoking in the bathroom.

Then there was the man the nurses called "12-Window," after the location of his bed. Now and then a high-volume string of profanities or a blood-curdling scream would echo down the hall, and a nurse would roll her eyes and say, "12-Window."

There's a medical term—"triage"—that comes from the care of

wounded in wartime. The rule is, the worst wounds get treated first. The walking wounded have to wait their turn. The only exception to that rule, on the battlefield, is when a soldier is so grievously wounded that he's going to die no matter how much attention he gets. In those cases, the medics relieve his pain and move on to treat those who may live to fight again.

Civilian hospitals practice triage, too. They have limited resources: there are only so many hours in a day, so many doctors and nurses, so many dollars to spend on medical care. Here in America, if you're wealthy or have good insurance, you probably won't have to wait very long to get treatment, but in other places that's not so. Though they may call it other things, like "health care rationing," it's triage.

Teachers practice a form of triage, too. There aren't enough hours in a day or week or school year to give all our students the kind of personal attention they—and their parents—crave. So we make choices.

Every teacher is different. Some give most of their attention to the high achievers, who are hard-working, eager to learn, and treat teachers with respect. Their families are involved, supportive, and helpful. Get a group like my honors freshmen together, and it's astounding what they can do. You can't wait to get to the classroom each day.

Others focus on the kids who are struggling to succeed. They're working hard and cooperating, but for whatever reason, learning doesn't come easily. Their families want to help but may not have the time or resources. Still, we'll go to absurd lengths to pull such kids through, and their achievements, if not as spectacular as others', are equally rewarding.

But some students are 12-Windows, the kind who can undermine an entire class. Their families, if we ever see them at all, may be abusive, even threatening. Then we each have a decision to make. Will we go on trying to reach that kid, spending our precious time and energy on what may be a lost cause? Or do we pull the plug? (6/9/05)

Boring

Last week, one of my favorite students in Honors Freshman English declared that the reflective essays we require our students to write had become "boring."

I was so shocked that I said something unforgivable: "What does that say about your life?"

I apologized later, and she was good enough to accept it. We were all feeling cranky last week. But I have to say—and I think I speak for all teachers when I do—that "boring" is a word that I hate to hear, and I hear it a great deal from students. My wife, who teaches fifth grade, has forbidden its use in her classroom. When Lisa Cochran, my co-teacher, hears it, she says, "Why don't you stop complaining and do something about it?"

The B-word is at once a complaint and an excuse. Loosely translated, it means, "You're not entertaining me, and that's why I'm not learning." It is the motto of the uninvolved, the battle cry of the passive. In our society, there is no social faux pas worse than being boring, and it appears to justify the most offensive behavior in response.

I witnessed this transaction at ConVal's graduation ceremonies last weekend. Okay, I agree that the graduation speech was tedious—overlong, self-involved, and neither thoughtful nor creative. And yes, the speaker actually invited the seniors to let him know by raising their hands when they felt—you know—so that he could move directly to the point of his speech.

I thought it was a risky invitation to issue, but they held out for a polite ten minutes before the first hands appeared. He ignored them. The audience laughed nervously. The hands went down. The speaker plowed on.

Ten more minutes went by, and the hands appeared again, more of them this time. The audience began raising their own hands. The speaker looked up, said, "soon, soon!" and went on. I leaned over to Cindy Dickinson, who teaches public speaking, and said, "He's lost the audience."

Ten more minutes dragged past. By now, some graduates were firing paper airplanes into the air, parts of the audience had begun a rhythmic clapping, and isolated voices could be heard imploring the speaker to cease. I had my head in my hands. I couldn't decide what was more embarrassing: the fatuousness of the speech or the discourtesy of the audience.

Finally—mercifully—it ended. There was a derisive ovation, and the ceremony went on. But it dampened what should have been a joyful occasion, and it left me feeling sad and worried.

One of the important reasons we attempt to educate young people is to give them the internal resources to cope with life's occasional stretches of tedium. Doctors put magazines in their waiting rooms because waiting for doctors is inevitable. Reading is a way to help the time pass more pleasantly. But it's no good if you can't read.

There are worse cases. History abounds with stories of prisoners—Saint Paul, Gandhi, Martin Luther King, Jr., Nelson Mandela, Senator John McCain—who kept their minds and spirits alive by thinking, reading, writing, reciting poetry, playing mental chess games, contemplating a better society. They were victims of an unjust world, but instead of stewing about it, they prepared themselves to change it.

So here's an extremely short graduation message, which I send with love and respect to the Class of 2005: Life isn't always entertaining. The real test of our education is what we choose to do about it. (6/23/05)

Sleeping in Class

One of my students fell asleep in class last week. It's not all that unusual. But the more I think about it, the more it seems like a story that might give you an idea of the kind of decisions a teacher faces every day.

This particular student—I'll call her Nancy—was stretched out on the floor of Room 215A during Modern Literature. She was there because we had devoted that day to working on a quilting project related to our reading. As a lot of my students have never made a quilt or even handled a needle and thread, they require a lot of time to sew together the four-square patch required for the project.

Those students who had already finished their patches were catching up on their reading assignment. But Nancy had not only finished her patch, she had also finished the book. In a large group of students (29), all of whom read at different speeds, it's common for some to finish ahead of the others. When they do, I tell them they can do other homework or read for pleasure—anything that doesn't disturb the rest of the class. Nancy chose to take a nap. I let her sleep.

I wasn't sure that was the right thing to do, so I asked some of the other teachers I know how they handle a sleeping student. One of them said she always wakes the student and asks if he or she needs to go to the school nurse. If the student says that's not necessary, she insists that the student remain awake. "It's a matter of fairness to others and respect for me," the teacher explained.

I see her point. In general, we shouldn't be encouraging students to sleep in school, and we should apply rules consistently. But there's something in me that rebels against that notion. I can't help remembering Emerson's dictum that "a foolish consistency is the hobgoblin of little minds."

When I was interviewed for this job, somebody asked me about my teaching philosophy. I began by saying it would be arrogant of me to claim to have one, never having been a teacher or studied educational philosophy. But I told the committee about a famous designer—I think it was Charles Eames—who, when asked what his design philosophy was, replied, "What's the problem?"

If I had to articulate a teaching philosophy, I would sound a lot like Eames: "Who's the student?" If Nancy falls asleep, all caught up with her work in a classroom where everyone was pursuing individual aims, where's the harm? However, if Nancy fell asleep during a group discussion or student presentation or, God forbid, one of my scintillating lectures, I would wake her up. I wake up sleeping students almost every day.

But even that policy admits exceptions. There have been students in my classes who were so disruptive that when I caught them sawing wood, as my mother used to say, I breathed a sigh of relief and tiptoed away. Perhaps I should have wakened them, but I knew that doing so would probably ignite a conflagration. All the other students would be distracted and the lesson plan shot to pieces, not to mention my composure.

Many years ago, when I was managing editor of *Yankee*, I said something pompous to my wife about all the difficult decisions I'd had to make that day, decisions involving thousands of dollars. She fired back that teachers make hundreds of decisions every day, each one of them difficult, and all of them involving the lives and prospects of children. As usual, she was right. But I didn't truly understand her until I became a teacher myself.

I still don't know if I did the right thing in letting Nancy sleep. I can see benefits in both approaches—one rule for everyone, or consider the circumstances in each case. When Nancy woke up, I mentioned my dilemma to her. She smiled and thanked me for not waking her. (11/3/05)

Ice Cream

When I started this job, one of my English Department colleagues, Cindy Dickinson, told me there would be good days and bad days, but one thing she could guarantee: it would never be dull. I've found that to be true. Lately, they're mostly good days, and one day last week, something happened in Freshman English that was so wonderful it alone made it a good week.

Just the day before, I had come into my second-block class, Classical Mythology, steaming. My freshmen had been so irritating that morning, I told my Mythies, that I really needed to play some games to turn around my mood.

The next day, though, I was talking to the freshmen about our new book, *The House on Mango Street* by Sandra Cisneros. It's short and deceptively simple, written in vignettes rather than chapters. Vignettes are incomplete stories—the name comes from French and refers to the practice of painters who did portraits without filling in the entire canvas, surrounding the portraits instead with little decorative vines. They're like snapshots, in a way, or freeze-frames from a video. A lot of my columns are vignettes, now that I think about it, including this one.

I was explaining that the vignettes were based on Cisneros's experiences growing up Latina in Chicago, but that they were fiction. Fiction is a tough concept for some ninth-graders. I asked one of my brightest students to define the term.

"Fiction is writing that is untrue," she said.

This tends to be the first answer whenever I ask that question, and I'm not willing to leave it alone. "Suppose something really happened to Cisneros when she was a girl, and she used that experience in a story, just the way it happened, except for changing the names," I said. "Is that untrue?"

They were stumped for a moment. Then one boy said, "Well, then they're nonfiction."

"But what if everything else in the same story has been changed?" I persisted. "In other words, part of the story really happened, but the rest didn't. Is it fiction or nonfiction?"

A number of my students started talking at once, but one girl, sitting in a corner, suddenly yelped, "I get it!"

I shushed the others. "What do you get?" I asked her.

Her face was shining. "It's like milk!"

That's when I knew something wonderful was about to happen.

"It's like milk," she continued. "If I brought in a quart of milk and told you it was milk, that would be true. If I brought in a carton of ice cream and said it was milk, that wouldn't be true. But there's milk in ice cream—it's just changed its form."

"So what you're saying," I said, "is that if you take milk and add flavorings, and maybe some preservatives, and put it in an ice-cream maker and freeze it, that's like what a writer does with her true experiences. What she produces after all those changes is fiction, but it still has truth in it, just like ice cream has milk. In fact, you can't make real ice cream without milk . . ."

"And you can't make fiction without truth," she finished.

When I went into Mythology a few minutes later, one of my students asked, "How were those freshmen today, Mr. Clark?"

"They were great," I said. "Let's see if you guys can do as well." (11/17/05)

[98]

Good Morning

According to last Sunday's *New York Times*, one out of three teachers has considered quitting, or knows another teacher who has considered quitting, because of rude students. The only surprise to me is that the numbers are so low.

Two weeks ago one of my colleagues was driven from her classroom in tears by sheer disrespect. She wasn't the first I've seen. Another, a veteran who I would have thought had survived the worst that disruptive students can hand out, went to administration last year to have one of his classes split up. He gave the students he thought might be salvaged to another teacher and kept the incorrigible savages in his own class. He sat them as far apart from each other as was physically possible and tried to teach them the rudiments of polite behavior. It didn't work.

In my horrible first year as a teacher, I considered quitting every day until April. Then, for reasons I still can't fully explain, I turned the corner. But the first seven months were an ordeal. I used to come back to my office from class and shake for minutes at a time. A couple of years ago, when another colleague in her first year was weeping at her desk (rude students), my friend Ann Moller went over to her and just stroked her hair for a second.

I said, "How come you never stroked my hair when I was having a bad day in my first year?"

Ann grinned. "You were shaking so hard I was afraid you'd hurt me," she said.

Why students behave so badly is a question I'll leave to the experts to try to explain. The good news is it's only a small minority who drive teachers to tears or early retirement.

The bad news is it's also only a small minority of students who are genuinely courteous. The vast middle group is neither utterly barbaric nor fully civilized.

Here's an example. One morning this fall, as students were on their way to their first classes, I came across Ann holding open one of the double doors in the hallway outside the English office. She caught my eye, and I came over.

"I've been counting," she said. "Seventy-seven students have gone through this door since I started holding it. Seven have said 'Thank you.'"

Recently, I have tried replicating her results. I now hold that same door open every morning before block one, because my classroom is close by, and we are expected to be in the halls to encourage good behavior.

The first week, my figures were very close to Ann's. Roughly one in ten students said "thank you" or otherwise acknowledged my help with a nod or a smile. Most of them were students I've had in class before.

Then I tried a new tack. I started saying "good morning" to all students who passed, whether I knew them or not. It felt a little artificial, but I persisted. At first, it didn't change anything, although I got a lot of startled looks from students who'd never been in my class.

However, in the second and third weeks of the experiment, something interesting has developed. I can't supply numbers—it's hard to count and say "good morning" at the same time—but I'm sure that the percentage of responses is increasing. I'm getting more smiles, more thanks, even a few tentative greetings in return. In fact, I'd guess it's approaching 50 percent.

It doesn't work all the time. A lot of students still trudge by without a glance; it's 7:30 in the morning, after all. I could offer them hundred-dollar bills and they wouldn't notice. But I've only gotten one hostile reaction to my charm offensive. It's a student in one of my classes, so I greet her by name. She looks me in the eye, curls her lip, and stalks past without speaking.

Somebody suggested I try reverse psychology and not speak to her at all. The trouble is, in order to do that, I'd have to act rudely. And if that's what it takes, maybe I'll find some other way to make a living. (12/1/05)

Not Reading

We were discussing Chapter Seven of *A Separate Peace* in Freshman English last week when suddenly one of my students raised his hand and said, "Mr. Clark, I haven't really read any of this book."

I can't say I was surprised. In the six and a half years I've been teaching, there have been many students who have let me know, directly or indirectly, that they haven't actually read the books they're supposed to be reading. And they weren't only freshmen. The funniest example came a few years ago when one senior chose to write about Kurt Vonnegut's *Slaughterhouse-Five* on his final exam. He praised it highly "except for the slaughterhouse scenes, which were too gory." (There are no gory scenes in the slaughterhouse, but it sure sounds like there ought to be, doesn't it?) Actually, it isn't funny at all. It's hard to teach literature to non-readers. Oh, most of them pass the courses. They're smart enough to pick up essential information from class discussion, or they read Cliff Notes, or they cheat. They're not dumb. They just can't read. In another burst of candor, a girl once complained that she didn't like the book we were reading because "the print is too small and the words are too big and there aren't any pictures."

Whenever this happens, I thank the student for his or her honesty. I make suggestions about how to stay awake while reading. I try the ideas in books on reading comprehension like *Strategies That Work* or *Mosaic of Thought*. In fact, I spent last Thursday in a workshop on reading comprehension. It was fascinating, and I'm eager to try some new ideas. But even there, the instructor agreed that for students who never learned the basics of reading—"decoding" is the term used by experts—strategies for deeper understanding are useless.

That's the problem with the boy in Freshman English, I think. I ask each student to stand up in front of the class and read a poem at least once in the quarter, and when he did, he struggled to sound out the words. He got them all right, but there was no fluency. It has to flow. It's like trying to hit a golf ball by thinking hard about each separate movement. I can assure you from bitter experience that it doesn't work.

So what do I do? He's not the only one in class with this problem. When I asked one of the girls why she hadn't been handing in the writing assignments that go with each chapter, she admitted, "I don't read very well." And another boy wrote a note on his last assignment: "Can you help me? I'm not getting this."

I've offered to stay after school for special tutoring, but they won't come. I could reconfigure the class into a group of fluent readers who work mostly on their own, while I spend more time with the slow readers. But I don't know how to teach decoding. It's a specialized skill. Or I could read the book out loud, stopping to ask questions and model my own reading strategies. I've done it with *The Odyssey*, and I'll do it again with *Romeo and Juliet.* But reading aloud won't help anyone learn to decode.

One obvious solution is to give those students who have trouble reading a complex novel something easier to read. But the funny thing is, even those students get something from this book. When we talk about it, they say smart things. Sometimes they understand it best of all.

I want all my students to be able to submerge themselves in a book, not just because it's a skill they'll need for the rest of high school and college, but because I believe it is a matter of life and death. *A Separate Peace* shows how fear makes us hurt the people we love best and how often we act on impulses that we regret for the rest of our lives. This is stuff they need to know, and they need to know it now, as adolescents, before one of those impulses wrecks their futures. I'm not sure that a book with bigger print and shorter words and pictures will teach it to them. (12/15/05)

Names and Faces

This is the time of year when a number of ConVal graduates who are on winter break from college stop by to say hello. One of them dropped in at the English office the other day and stood there, smiling expectantly.

It was awkward. Jill Lawler and I had both had her in classes, but neither of us could come up with her name. Jill finally took the bullet. "Your face is familiar," she said, "but I can't place the name."

The student graciously identified herself. "I couldn't remember your name either," I admitted. "But I remember a poem you wrote in my Creative Writing class. It was about putting together a jigsaw puzzle, how you have to start with the edge pieces."

She looked surprised and pleased. "I remember that poem! It turned out to be about figuring out who you are."

"It was a good poem," I said. "The final line was something like, 'and the last piece is always sky.'"

My memory grows less reliable every day, but for some reason I retain these shards of language. I can walk down the halls at ConVal, cataloging the familiar but nameless faces: "She wrote the poem about cowboy boots, because she moved here from Texas, and he's the one who wrote the funny story about being a teenage vampire, and that's the guy who wrote about writer's block. He said it was like standing outside a locked house, looking in the windows."

Sometimes it's a name, not a face, that triggers the memories. The other day somebody mentioned a student who has done great things as a chef since graduating from our culinary arts program. He brought her up as an example of a student who followed a non-traditional career pathway.

But I remember her as one of my favorite poets. She couldn't spell at all and her punctuation was shaky, but she had an eye and a voice and an overflowing heart, which is all a poet really needs.

Then there are the astounding talents, like Claire Villeneuve, whom I recognized at The Bagel Mill a few weeks ago as she was smearing cream cheese on my toasted poppy-seed. At first, I wasn't sure it was her, but my brain was reeling with lines and images from her poems—the foot going through the drywall and the graffiti under the bridge.

"Are you still writing?" I asked her.

"Yes, some," she said.

"Good!" I said with more vehemence than I intended, and she looked startled.

This is the last week of the first semester. Next week, I'll have to start learning a hundred new names and faces. The old ones, the names I learned last fall, will go back into my faulty memory banks, where many of them will disappear. Afterward, all that will remain of them, perhaps, will be their indelible stories: his first deer, the 1,200-pound Belgian horse she loved and trained, the prom date who broke his heart, and the summer she left home to join a traveling carnival. (1/26/06)

Open House

A few weeks ago there was an article in the *New York Times* about a study showing that, while students from private schools, including charter schools, generally outperform students in public schools, if those results are adjusted for family income, they are reversed. In other words, if the student body of Saint Paul's School walked down the street to Concord High School, and vice versa, Concord High's test scores would outstrip those of the venerable prep school.

This is no surprise. Research has consistently shown that the best predictor of a student's success is the income and educational level of his or her parents. There are exceptions, of course; I did well in school although we were not wealthy and neither of my parents went to college. There are also examples of students who fail in spite of the best advantages.

But the fact remains: students whose parents are well-educated and financially secure enough to supply their child with preschool experience, books, computers, internet access, summer enrichment programs, and other educational resources do better in school than those whose parents are too poor or too busy making a living to help out.

On a local level, I see evidence of this every time we have an open house at ConVal, which we did last week. I came out of it, as I always do, with mixed feelings. I'm elated by the excitement of talking about the job and the subject I love. It's a great opportunity to thank parents for their hard work and their commitment to public schooling. It's also depressing to see so few of the parents whose kids are not succeeding.

The Freshman Honors English class I co-teach with Lisa Cochran has 45 students in all, and we probably had 50 parents come to open house. The timing was dicey: we had just handed back the first writing assignment. As an experiment, we had asked them to evaluate their own work before handing it in, and the lowest self-assessment I saw in my half of the class was 87. That happened to be the highest grade I gave out. The rest were 20 to 30 points lower than the self-assessment, possibly the lowest grades these students had ever received. Lisa's results were virtually identical.

So we were braced for a parental firestorm. It never came. They were friendly and supportive. There were some questions about our methods, but they were reasonable and polite.

The next class was Journalism: 20 students, sophomores to seniors, from all levels of educational attainment. Three parents showed up, representing two students. They were nice people, their students are doing well, and we had a good talk. Five of the students in that class are currently failing the course, but they were not represented.

The third class was another Freshman English class, but not the honors group. It's just 21 nice kids, covering the gamut from enthusiasm to indifference. Again, we had a lovely talk. Five parents or relatives were there, representing three students.

I know that failing to come to open house does not make one a bad parent, any more than showing up qualifies one for sainthood. There are dozens of good reasons why overworked parents might not want to rush through dinner and get dressed up to go back to high school for a couple of hours. And it's not as if open house is much of an opportunity for serious discussion of a student's problems and prospects: it's a dog-and-pony show.

But the message I want to send to parents is this: your child's education, in a public school, will be exactly as good as you are willing to make it. It's not something teachers do to your child. It's something you, the teacher, and most important, your child, do together. (3/9/06)

My First Field Trip

I've been teaching nearly seven years now, and I took a class on a field trip for the first time a couple of weeks ago. It was to RiverMead, the retirement community in Peterborough: about five miles, round-trip.

A friend from Dublin who lives there now had asked me to come address the residents about my concern, expressed in this space, that boys seem to be lagging behind girls academically at ConVal and across the nation. I was willing, but the day and time he wanted me to come, I had a Journalism class.

So I decided to take the class with me. After all, who would know more about how boys and girls respond differently to high school than the boys and girls themselves? Plus, they could write stories about the event for the school newspaper.

I checked with my RiverMead friend to see if that would be all right. He was intrigued and got it cleared at his end. I filled out the necessary forms at my end, handed out permission slips to my 20 students, and reminded them every day for a week that we were going on a field trip on Monday and that the bus would leave at 9:45 sharp, with or without them. Six of them were either absent, cut class, or forgot about the trip. Five of the six were boys.

We arrived to find an audience of about a hundred residents. I made a few remarks, then I put the four boys who made the trip on stage. RiverMead had provided a handheld wireless microphone for us, and I was ready to ask the kids questions myself if the residents were too shocked or shy, but that was not necessary. There were hands up in the audience for the entire hour.

We didn't stick strictly to the subject. I had contemplated asking my students to dress more formally than normal for the visit, but on reflection, decided that our audience should see high school students in their native plumage—unedited, uncensored, unretouched. I suspect this was why one of the first questions was, "Does your high school have a dress code?"

When we got around to gender and schools, one of the boys

said that boys have "higher priorities" than academics—sports, mainly. Another explained that boys who got good grades ran the risk of being called "kiss-ups." Someone in the audience asked for a definition of the term, which led to a minor semantic skirmish. I translated "kiss-up" as a derogatory term for a student who curries favor with teachers, but one of the girls denied it. She said it was a term of respect for "someone who works really hard."

One of the boys offered to put it in context. "Say I call a guy up on a Saturday to see what he's doing, and he says he's studying," he explained. "So I'd say, 'don't be such a kiss-up!'"

After the boys were done, I brought four girls up on stage to get their perspective. They agreed that boys had other things on their minds. More interestingly, they said that when they were younger, they also tried to avoid looking too smart for fear of being unpopular. "Guys like to teach girls stuff," one said, "so I'd pretend not to know anything." But they all agreed that as they matured, they stopped doing that. "Now girls just work harder."

I've left out a lot. The hour went by swiftly, and as we departed, one of the residents said, "I wish it could have gone on all morning." My friend called later to say that everyone who attended was still talking about it, and many wanted to invite us back for more.

That was gratifying. But the best part was the five-minute ride back to ConVal on the bus. The students talked passionately about the experience all the way, and when we got into class, they didn't stop for another hour.

It was only five miles, but you don't have to go very far to find a different world. I must do this more often. (4/20/06)

[108]

Appreciation

Next week is Teacher Appreciation Week. That means a discount at the Toadstool Bookstore, for which I'm grateful. Otherwise, there's not much to it, and that's fine with me. The best form of teacher appreciation comes from students and their parents, and they're usually too busy, too embarrassed, or too—well, unappreciative—to make a big deal of it.

But every now and then I get a letter like the one that came last week from a former student. "Dear Mr. Clark," it began. "You may not remember me, but a few years ago I was a student of yours."

Not remember her? Fat chance. She was one of the sharpest, wittiest, most original minds I've had the pleasure to try to mold. She discarded her given name for one she liked better while she was in high school, and she's still using it. Let's call her Molly.

Molly was an unsettling presence in a classroom—never disruptive or disrespectful, but sphinx-like. Her silences had weight. I first encountered her in the fall of 2000, when she was in my Survey of American Literature class. She sat by herself, hardly ever spoke, avoided eye contact, and barely concealed her contempt for her dunder-headed classmates. She was, however, kind and generous with another outsider, a girl whose struggles with writing were painful to watch.

Molly had no such problem—she was easily the best writer in the class, and she delighted in challenging every assumption I threw out, even if it meant accepting an F on a paper whose assigned topic she regarded as contemptible. I am making her sound obnoxious, and I suppose that she was to some teachers, who couldn't understand why she wouldn't answer to the name clearly printed on their class rosters.

But American literature is filled with people reinventing themselves, and I loved having her in class. Molly breezed through American Lit., then came back in the spring to take Mythology with me. Once again, she operated in a soundproof bubble, but her hand-made illustrated book of mythological parodies was so good I took it home and put it on my bookshelf.

I wrote her a college recommendation (from which I am pilfering much of what you just read), she graduated, and I haven't seen her in five years. Then came the letter, which I found in my mail slot and read first thing Monday morning.

"I guess this is a strange sort of letter to receive, but I just wanted to say I really appreciated your efforts and kindness to me. I guess kids mostly brush off the things people do for them when they're younger—after all, the world is all about us—but sometimes we fail in being totally self-centered. Rude to be so out of character, I know. Well, assignments are over for me, but hopefully they will not be over for you for quite some time. Maybe you can get a few more kids to be out of character."

That's a good way to start a week. However, before applying for sainthood, I did some calculating. Somewhere among the faces in my classroom this semester is my 1,000th student since I began teaching seven years ago. Out of those thousand students, I've probably received a dozen letters like Molly's. I keep them in a file folder on the advice of a colleague, who said I'd need to look at them after bad days. She was right. They make me feel like I'm not a hopeless fraud.

On the other hand, 12 nice letters out of a thousand students is an Appreciation Average of 1.2 percent. Maybe I am a hopeless fraud. At least I haven't received any hate mail from former students (yet).

I don't feel neglected, though, and this is not a plea for sympathy. I get a paycheck every two weeks, and the health insurance is excellent. Lots of students have thanked me verbally, smiled at me in the halls, or best of all, taken another class or two of mine. Parents say nice things, too.

Toss in the Toadstool discount, and it's a pretty good deal. (5/4/06)

A Ten-Minute Window

I was rude to the mother of one of my students last week. She was upset enough to call my principal, Sue Dell, and ask for a meeting of the three of us at 7:00 the next morning. Here's how it happened.

I had been ordered to attend an IEP meeting on Monday afternoon at the end of the day. An IEP is an Individualized Education Program, designed by special educators in collaboration with an identified student's family, to make whatever accommodations or modifications are necessary to give that student a fair chance to succeed in class. ConVal has more than 200 students with IEPs.

This quarter, out of the 75 students I'm directly responsible for, I have only two students with IEPs. Some teachers have many more. Also, because we're approaching the end of the year, there are more and longer IEP meetings than usual, as new and revised plans are being written for next school year.

So there I was at the meeting at 2:30. I had another meeting to attend at 3:00, at the district office, but I figured I might be done in time to get to it. I watched the clock and checked the lengthy document we were discussing to see when my turn would come. There did not appear to be anything in the document about English class, and the student was doing fine in my class, but I figured there might be questions I could answer.

There weren't. At 3:05, I raised my hand and said, "I don't wish to be rude, but why am I here?"

A special educator explained that the federal law governing special education said one of the student's regular teachers had to be present—and for the whole meeting.

Luckily, there was another teacher at the meeting who asked if his presence could satisfy the law's requirements. After some discussion, it was agreed that I could leave. As I got up, my student's mother said, "Wait!" She dug under the table and brought out a gift-wrapped box and handed it to me. I apologized for my haste, thanked her, and left.

The next morning, in Sue's office, after praising and thanking me for the work I'd done with her student, the mother looked right at me and said, "What have we done to make you so disgruntled with us?"

I apologized again. "I wasn't disgruntled with you," I added. "You're one of my favorite parents and your son is one of my favorite students. I was disgruntled with the situation."

She accepted my apology and went on to tell us, with heartbreaking eloquence, how hard it is to have a child with a disability: the unrelenting anxiety, the constant need to be vigilant and to speak up on the child's behalf and—this was the main point—the frustration of seeing regular educators like me acting as if her child were an inconvenience.

These weren't her exact words, but they're close: "We hate feeling like a stepchild, a burden on these overworked professionals," she said. "Is there any way," she added, turning to Sue, "to let your regular educators know, to help them understand, how much we need their input? How important it is that we feel like members of a team? I know how pressed for time you all are. If we could have even a ten-minute window, it would help so much."

It made me feel small. But the cruel fact is that there are so many competing demands on a teacher's time, especially in the final weeks of school, that any mandatory meeting, especially one in which the teacher's presence may have little real value, is an inconvenience. It is a burden.

Worse, it is not an opportunity for real reflection. It is not an opportunity to truly gain insight into the needs of students and their families. Those things would require the kind of time and energy that none of us have as school rushes to an end. (And, by the way, if we're serious about educational reform, let's talk about year-round schooling.)

But the law is the law. So we go to mandatory meetings and fill out forms. "That's what teachers do now," one of my colleagues said recently. "We fill out forms." Recently, a frustrated person in the main office went on the public address system after school, threatening to withhold paychecks from teachers if she didn't get the forms she needed. I don't blame her: she had forms to fill out, too.

I don't mean to single out IEP meetings. Special educators are the firefighters of public education, genuine heroes. I could have mentioned the meetings on curriculum reform, the meetings on changing student behavior, the meetings about schoolwide rubrics. Then there are the standardized tests, the concerts, the dinners, the special awards assemblies, the end-of-the-semester field trips, or any one of a dozen other items spilling off the agenda. Taken one at a time, each is important, even praiseworthy. Put them all together, they spell chaos. In this deranged environment, even a ten-minute window might be too much to ask. And that's a shame.

Still, none of that excuses my rudeness to that mother. I felt even worse when I opened the gift she gave me. It was a beautiful blue coffee mug bearing the words "Nice Guy." (6/15/06)

Relevance

When I was in college, I wanted to be a reporter, so I eagerly signed up for a course called "Politics and Mass Media." It was worthless. On the other hand, I took one called "Western Thought and Institutions" only because my roommate talked me into it. It was the best course I took. You can't tell the value of a course by what it's called.

I thought of that during our Curriculum Committee's four-month investigation of ConVal's graduation requirements. Parents, School Board members, and especially students kept insisting that what ConVal teaches our children needs to be relevant to their lives.

Let's look in the dictionary to learn something about the meaning and history of the word "relevant." (I'm an English teacher. We love dictionaries. When my own kids used to ask about a word, I'd say, "Let's look in the dictionary," and they'd moan.)

"Relevant" is defined by Webster's as "having significant and demonstrable bearing upon the matter at hand." Synonyms include germane, pertinent, and applicable, which seems closest to what those who press for relevance in schooling mean. They want students to be taught things they can apply to their lives. That fits nicely with the Latin root of the word, *relevare*, which means to lift up or lighten a burden. Make it useful, they're saying.

For many areas of learning, the practical value is obvious. We all need to know how to read, write, speak, listen, add, subtract, multiply, divide, and so on. That's been true for millennia. In our time, students also need higher math, an understanding of the scientific method, knowledge and appreciation of history, geography, and economics, as well as exposure to foreign cultures and languages. The Curriculum Committee has recommended adding courses on health and career planning as well.

It's trickier to make the case for the practical value of subjects like art and music, which is why those subjects are so often the first to be abandoned when school districts cut back. I don't have the space here to argue why those are not only relevant, but essential. Instead, I'll tell you about one of my own courses, Classical Mythology, which at first glance appears to have no practical value at all. Many might dismiss it as fluff.

Classical Mythology is the study of the Greek and Roman myths. It's a popular course; I've probably had more students take Myth than anything else I teach. That's because it's fun. Myths by definition are entertaining stories, or else they wouldn't have endured for thousands of years. It doesn't hurt that, as I warn my students on the first day of class, they include a lot of sex and violence. I offer any student who wants to avoid discussion of sex and violence a chance to drop the class right then. Strangely, not one has taken me up on it.

But how is it practical? On their final exams, I ask my students to describe what they have learned about myths, life, and themselves during the course. One boy, who flunked the course, startled me by writing, "I think all students should be required to take Myth. This class makes you think in depth about other cultures' beliefs. It also helps you to uncover your talents and overcome your fears."

Another boy wrote, "The Hercules myth intrigues me because it reminds me of myself. Everything from the great strength to the wild emotions and constant need for atonement fits me to a T. Through analyzing this myth, I have learned better to control myself."

Is that fluff? I prefer to think of it as relevant: it lifts students up and lightens their burdens. Maybe we should rename the course. We could use the words the Greeks chiseled into the temple of the oracle of Apollo: "Know Thyself." (6/29/06)

Summer School

Every teacher ought to go back to school now and then, if only to remind ourselves how hard it is to be a student. I spent the month of July in Washington, DC, at the Teaching Shakespeare Institute, a program run by the Folger Shakespeare Library under the auspices of the National Endowment for the Humanities. It was exciting, exhausting, and humbling.

I did a different NEH program five years ago at Yale. But where that was a leisurely ramble through the Middle Ages with Chaucer's Canterbury pilgrims—we met three days a week, for two hours a session, and wrote no papers—this was more like a cavalry charge. Five mornings a week we mounted a yellow school bus that took us from our Georgetown University dormitory to the Folger Library on Capitol Hill, where we spent eight hours listening to lectures, chewing them over in seminars, collecting and creating lesson plans, writing research papers, and learning from experts how to perform Shakespeare on stage, from soliloquies to swordfights.

We were 25 high school teachers from all over the country. We averaged 6.5 years of teaching (although individual experience ranged from two years to more than 30), we represented high schools public and private averaging 1,184 students (almost precisely the number of students at ConVal), and in age—well, let's just say that a majority of my colleagues could have been my children. They included a 295-pound football coach from Texas, an Orthodox rabbi-in-training from New York, and a tough-as-nails field hockey coach from Pennsylvania who, on our first night, coolly rattled off the names of every participant, including faculty and staff, who had just been introduced. Fast company.

For the first week, I felt overmatched. Our first assignment was to write a short paper based on primary sources from the Folger's vast holdings. (Example: the Folger owns 72 copies of Shakespeare's First Folio. The next largest collection in the world, at the University of Tokyo, has 15.)

Part of the assignment included a research log. Mine began

thusly: "July 7—Not a good day. Opened my musical laptop in the Reading Room, earning glares from a dozen PhDs. Didn't know how to stop the music, so I shut it down and fled."

I had trouble not only with my borrowed laptop but with the art of original research, which I hadn't done since the Nixon Administration. The librarians and our resident scholars were gracious and helpful, but I was in full panic mode. Finally, I decided to junk the suggested areas of inquiry for something more familiar: the weather. There's an awful lot of violent weather in *Macbeth, Julius Caesar,* and *The Tempest,* the three plays we were assigned. How did people of Shakespeare's era (1564–1616) explain lightning, thunder, and other atmospheric phenomena?

It turned out to be a good topic and one not frequently studied. I managed to crank out a paper that the scholars liked, and I learned that thunder on Wednesdays was once thought to portend "the death of harlots." I found a 1606 almanac that reminded me of the familiar yellow publication I've been writing for since 1978 and got goosebumps when I saw a note written in the margins of a book published in 1584 that exactly paralleled my own thoughts when I read it 422 years later.

From that point on, I was okay. But it was a valuable lesson. When I return to ConVal later this month and start assigning papers, I'm going to remember that sick-to-my-stomach feeling of inadequacy, the 3:00 a.m. anxiety attacks, and my conviction that I was the dumbest person in the class. It's easy to forget how often we've all felt stupid and awkward in school. (8/10/06)

A Clean, Well-Lighted Place

The ConVal English Department is trying a new approach to dealing with students who have trouble with the basics of reading, writing, and speaking. We've created an 18-week course called English Competency, and we're going to teach it in three-person teams, each person specializing in one of those three areas. We're hoping that the novelty of having three different teachers, each one for only six weeks at a time, will help those students be more successful.

I'm going to teach reading. One of the problems some students have with reading is, as one of them told me, "there are too many long words and too many pages." Hand such students a 275-page novel with small print and no pictures, and they get discouraged right away. Even breaking it up into ten-page increments doesn't help. After trying hard for a few days, most of them give up.

So my approach will be to concentrate on short stories, which we can read together and complete in one class. That's why I spent the last two weeks of the summer reading Hemingway's short stories. Most of them aren't very long, and he's famous for using short words. I hadn't read any of them since high school, when Mr. Teunis, the teacher who had the most to do with me becoming the person I am now, read us "Cat in the Rain."

He was a formidable-looking figure, the first teacher I'd ever seen with a beard. I remember him pointing at students that day, asking them to stand up and say something about the story. We were all terrified, and most of us had nothing to say. When he pointed at me, I stood up and croaked something.

He stared at me, then said, "What is your name, please?"

I'm doomed, I thought, and told him my name.

"Mr. Clark, that is the first intelligent comment I've heard today," he said, and I was hooked.

One of his favorite stories was "A Clean, Well-Lighted Place." It's about two waiters in a little Spanish cafe, who are waiting for the last customer, an old man, to finish his drink so they can close up.

One of the waiters is annoyed with the customer, because he wants to go out. The other, older waiter, is more sympathetic. When the customer finally leaves, the older waiter offers to lock up so that the younger man can go. As he's cleaning up, he reflects on the refuge a clean, well-lighted place like the cafe offers, not just from the falling dark, but from *nada*, a word that means "nothing" but also stands for emptiness, chaos, an indifferent universe.

Nada, Mr. Teunis explained, is always around us. It is boredom, anxiety, dread, inadequacy, despair. When threatened by *nada*, we all need a clean, well-lighted place, and it's different for each of us. For Mr. Teunis, it was the weekend cabin he had on the Shenandoah River. He even named it "A Clean, Well-Lighted Place." Ironically, it was the place he died, when he dived into the river to try to save a person who was drowning.

For me, it's any place with a comfortable chair, a reading light, and a book. For another, it might be the family dinner table, a shopping mall, a golf course, or a sofa in front of the TV.

But it's more than a physical place: it's a feeling of security, of hope, of orderliness, of self-worth. It's my home. It's my wife and my children and my dog. It's the feeling I got 40 years ago when Mr. Teunis told me I'd said something smart.

I suspect that some of the students I'll be finding in English Competency don't often have those feelings in school, and they need them to succeed. The task ahead of me—of all teachers—is to see if we can make a clean, well-lighted place in our classrooms. (9/7/06)

[119]

Make It Fun

I learned a dance called the Funky Chicken from Roger Squitero, a classmate of mine at John F. Kennedy High School in Wheaton, Maryland, in 1968. He didn't actually teach it to me; I just watched him and practiced at home. I never performed it in public, unless you count trying to teach it to my granddaughter, Annie, last summer, in front of her parents and her grandmother, who were doubled over with laughter. Annie has the wing-flaps down cold, but she needs more work on her head-bobbing.

A couple of weeks ago I had another opportunity to do the Funky Chicken, this time in front of my Freshman English class. We were doing Teacher for a Minute, which I've written about before. It's often funny and, on occasion, deeply moving. I remember one year a girl with severe hearing loss, who almost never spoke in class, stood up and said, "I guess it's time to talk about my hearing." Then she pulled her hearing aid out of her head. We were riveted. "How far does that thing go in?" somebody asked.

Nothing so dramatic has happened in this class so far, but we just got started. I have learned some interesting things, though. On the day in question, a sweet little blond girl volunteered to teach us all the Crip Walk. For those of you not current on teenage slang, this is not a disrespectful slur against the physically challenged. It's worse. The Crips are a gang of thugs, dope dealers, and killers that started on the West Coast and, along with their deadly rivals, the Bloods, have spread their tentacles across the country.

At first I was startled that 15-year-olds from small-town New Hampshire were familiar with the dance preferences of LA drug lords. Then I was bemused by the idea that Crips might actually do the Crip Walk. I didn't think gangsters danced except in *West Side Story*.

My students, however, assured me this was the genuine item and went on to demonstrate their mastery of a hand signal alleged to represent membership in the Bloods. Just about everyone in class knew how to do it, too—lots more than the number who knew anything about, say, pronoun-antecedent agreement or how to avoid a comma fault.

Gang lore is, for better or worse (I'd say worse), a lot cooler than grammar lore if you're 15 years old. Gangsters, by extension, are way cooler than English teachers. It was at this point that I considered deploying the Funky Chicken. Then I remembered a fire drill on a bitterly cold day a few years ago, when I recommended that my class stay warm by dancing. I put a few moves on them, and one girl made a face. "No old-man dancing!" she said.

I bring all this up to illustrate the vast, abyssal gap between the generations. Preferences in dancing don't matter much, though. What does matter are attitudes about learning. Last week another member of that class complained that she wasn't having any fun in English. I said I wasn't hired to entertain or amuse my students.

"But you're supposed to make it fun!" she insisted, and most of the class agreed with her. And therein, dear reader, lies the crux of the problem. Many of our children come to school believing that teachers must make learning fun. They have a constitutional right not to be bored. If they are bored, it's because the teacher is incompetent or the material being taught is dumb.

I'm trying to teach them a new idea: That if they are bored, it's not because *The Odyssey* is dumb, as one of my freshmen once told me. It's because they don't understand it. That's fine: nobody understands *The Odyssey* the first time around. But I'd prefer that they say, "I don't understand this," so that we can figure it out together, which can be a lot of fun.

And if that doesn't work, there's always the Funky Chicken. (11/30/06)

[121]

Obi-Wan Fails

For years, when my freshmen were noisy I stood at the front of the room, closed my eyes, and pretended to be Obi-Wan Kenobi, the sage of the original Star Wars films. Using The Force, I reached out toward the worst sources of clamor and mimed collecting them, pulling them inward, rolling them between my hands like balls of clay to make them smaller, until they disappeared.

It looked like I'd lost my mind, but it always worked, until now. The first time I tried it on my current freshman class, somebody yelled, "Look, he's pretending to be Obi-Wan!" The spell was broken, and they went on gabbing.

This freshman class is the rowdiest, most immature, most disrespectful bunch I've seen since my first year as a teacher. I'm not alone, either. I've heard the same thing from teachers in other subjects, too.

First, they are rude. They talk constantly—when I'm speaking, when other students are speaking, during silent reading time, even during movies. I've made class rules, I've handed out detentions, I've called parents, I've assigned seats, I've reassigned seats, I've shouted, I've whispered, I've remained silent. Nothing has worked.

It's not just the talking, either. They are nasty to each other, and they have a wildly exaggerated idea of their rights. When I intercepted a note being passed in class, the writer accused me of stealing her personal property.

But that's adolescence. What's more worrisome is a stony refusal to try anything that's difficult or challenging. Ask them to do something they haven't done before, and they frequently say, "I don't get it."

"I don't get it" doesn't mean, "please help me understand." It means "I don't want it, I won't listen, I don't care, go away." "I don't get it" is a brick wall, and my forehead is getting bloody.

Last week I was trying to get my freshmen to read *Romeo and*

Juliet. It's hard, I acknowledged, but most of the words Shakespeare used mean just the same today as they did 400 years ago. I put the students in groups and asked them to read a scene line by line. If any member of the group understands the line, I said, that person should explain it to the rest. If you come to a line that nobody understands, ask me for help.

One girl wasn't even looking at her book. "What line don't you understand?" I asked her.

"All of them," she replied sullenly, looking down at the table.

Over the last week or so, I've been asking various people why they think this is happening. My juniors and seniors think it's because the freshmen have no respect for their elders, i.e., juniors and seniors. "I learned stuff from upperclassmen when I was a freshman," one of them said. "But I can't tell these guys anything."

My son Joel thinks it might be technology—iPods, Instant Messaging, YouTube, Facebook. "They are so good at multitasking, they don't know how to concentrate on one thing," he commented.

Stephanie Brock, the wise woman who cuts my hair, thinks it is the collapse of families. "Nobody eats together as a family," she pointed out. "Kids come home to empty houses after school."

Mel Allen, who started working at *Yankee* about the same time I did and is now its editor, says young people don't read anymore. He's teaching a class at UMass for senior journalism majors, and when he asked them to name their favorite nonfiction writers, none of his students could name even one. "They're just months from trying to find jobs as journalists," he marveled, "and they don't read journalism!"

It's not every freshman, of course. But I fear we have reached a tipping point, a place where just enough of them have gone over to the Dark Side to intimidate the boys and girls who genuinely want to learn. And even Obi-Wan can't seem to stop it. (1/11/07)

It's About You

I've always loved losing myself in a book. I may have been the only seventh-grade boy in history who loved "Evangeline," and I can still recite the opening lines. I was lucky to have good English teachers who took me from *Great Expectations* to *Catch-22*. One of them, Bill Teunis, talked me into quitting the football team to be in a play called *King Lear*.

It would be nice to think that all American children have experiences like mine, but we know that's not true. I asked my freshmen this fall to bring in favorite books from home, books they find easy to read, for a few minutes of sustained silent reading each day. Research shows that for struggling readers, the best way to increase fluency, comprehension, and word recognition is to read books at or below their grade level.

Most of my kids brought in books, but about half a dozen did not. They said they forgot. After they forgot for a week or so, I realized there were no favorite books at home. So I borrowed a few dozen books from my wife, who teaches fourth- and fifth-graders, and brought them to school for my reluctant readers.

Fewer and fewer children read at home. According to a 2004 study by the National Endowment for the Arts, only 57 percent of all Americans read any kind of literature—fiction, poetry, plays—at all. Dana Gioia, chairman of the Endowment, said at the time that "Reading is in decline among all groups, in every region, at every educational level, and within every ethnic group" in America. The steepest decline is among young adults ages 18–24.

And maybe that's okay. As my old college English professor Kevin Starr said, if 57 percent of Americans occasionally read literature, that's not bad. "You can get through American life and be very successful," he told the *New York Times*, "without anybody ever asking you whether Shylock is an anti-Semitic character or whether *Death in Venice* is better than *The Magic Mountain*."

That's true. But it's also true, as Freud once said, that "only in the realm of fiction can we encounter the multiplicity of lives we need to understand our own." I don't teach literature, as one of my ConVal colleagues put it, in order to produce more English teachers. I teach literature because I think it's the best way to prepare my students to become decent, caring, honorable husbands and wives, mothers and fathers, employees and employers, neighbors and citizens.

I truly believe that I am better prepared to understand the terrors and wonders of my life because Bill Teunis gave me Shakespeare and Kevin Starr gave me Willa Cather. I understand now what General James Gavin, one of the heroes of World War II, meant when he told me in an interview that he'd learned more about leadership from *Madame Bovary* than from West Point.

When my students read *Death of a Salesman*, I ask them whether Willy Loman is a good father or a small-minded tyrant; whether Linda Loman is a loving wife or an enabler; and when is Biff Loman going to stop blaming his miseries on his father and start taking responsibility for his own life? I want my freshmen to see that their first year at ConVal is as thrilling and dangerous a journey as that of Odysseus trying to get home from the Trojan War. It's about you, I tell them. *The Odyssey* is about you, and *Romeo and Juliet* is about you, and even *Black Boy* is about you, though 98 percent of you here in New Hampshire are white.

I want them to know the pleasure of losing yourself in a book— and the even greater pleasure of finding yourself in one. (1/25/07)

The Wrong Obi-Wan

One of the most interesting letters I got in response to my column about last semester's freshman class pointed out that the problem with my Obi-Wan impression may have been that my Obi-Wan is a different fellow than my students' Obi-Wan. "Teens perceive Obi-Wan as a brash young Ewan McGregor rather than the stately Alec Guinness," my correspondent wrote. "Perhaps this is part of their problem?"

Maybe so. It's certainly part of my problem. Being approximately 40 years older than my students, my pop-culture references are likely to waft over their heads. I'll never forget the time I showed the 1967 film *Cool Hand Luke* to my Modern Literature class. They were skeptical at first ("Is this movie in color, Mr. Clark?"), but who can resist a character who eats 50 hard-boiled eggs in one hour?

When it was over, one girl said she really liked the actor who played Luke.

"That's Paul Newman," I said.

"The salad dressing guy?" she said in astonishment.

The reverse is also true. When I asked my Creative Writing class to write about a Christmas present they always wanted but never got, I didn't recognize any of the toys except for the venerable E-Z-Bake Oven. They were incredulous.

But it's not just pop culture. I have to constantly remind myself that my students are often ignorant of basic information about history, science, and economics. Recently I had one of my classes read Hemingway's short story "Cat in the Rain." I chose it for two reasons: one is that Hemingway uses mostly short words and simple sentence structure. The other reason was that it was "Cat in the Rain" we were reading in 1967 when my favorite teacher, Mr. Teunis, called on me for the first time, and I managed to say something smart.

We actually had a moment like that in my class. Briefly, the story is about a young American couple in an Italian hotel. The wife notices a cat outside in the rain, and she goes down to rescue it. The cat has disappeared, so she goes back to her room and complains to her husband that she wants a cat to hold on her lap and stroke. He tells her to find something to read. Then the door opens, and a maid offers the young woman a different cat, which the padrone, the owner of the hotel, has found for her.

"What does the young woman really want, besides a cat?" I asked my students. After a few desultory efforts, one boy said, "Maybe she wants a baby?"

I praised him fervently, then asked, "Why did the padrone send the young woman a cat?"

"He wanted to sleep with her," a different boy said.

"Really?" I said. "This elderly Italian man tries to seduce a young American woman with a cat?"

They all agreed. Why else would he have sent it?

"How many of you have ever stayed in a hotel?" I asked. A few hands went up. "Have any of you ever actually paid for a hotel room?" No hands. So I explained about paying for the room and food, and how it's traditional to leave a tip for good service.

"Isn't it more likely that the padrone wanted a bigger tip?" I asked. "Or that he just wanted his guest to be happy?"

No, they said. He wanted to sleep with her.

I don't know which is more depressing: that they couldn't imagine doing something nice for someone without being compensated for it, or that the compensation necessarily must be sex. But then, I'm Alec Guinness, not Ewan McGregor. (2/18/07)

Caught Up in the Game

Last Monday a troubled young man at Virginia Tech murdered 32 people. Within a day or two, we were told he was an English major, and that he had submitted violent, gory work in a creative writing course—work so dark and horrific that his teacher sent copies to administrators and urged that her student receive counseling. Apparently, nothing ever came of her request.

Every English teacher must confront the issue of violent imagery in student writing. Just a few weeks ago, two boys in one of my classes responded to what I thought was an innocent writing prompt—"What's your favorite carnival ride?"—with shocking fantasies about blowing up the rides and beheading the people who go to carnivals.

"It was just a joke!" one of them said when I told them I would show their responses to administrators. I replied that we can't permit such jokes in the world we now live in, any more than an airplane passenger is permitted to joke about carrying a bomb on board.

I don't think either of those boys will ever commit heinous acts. But how can I be sure? Nobody thought Seung-Hui Cho would gun down his teachers and fellow students. Nobody thought the Columbine killers were serious, even when they posted their plans on the internet.

The fact is that our high schools—including ConVal—contain many young men with violent fantasies. Some are troubled loners, like Cho. Some brag about their knowledge of weaponry, like the boy who stabbed another student to death at Lincoln-Sudbury High School in Massachusetts recently. Some are just ordinary kids with a taste for video games and movies that reek of blood and gore. The stories I gave to the administration weren't much worse than writing I've seen in other classes.

Shakespeare reeks of blood and gore, too. Once, when I was reading aloud from Tim O'Brien's Vietnam novel *The Things They Carried*, I became aware that a girl was sobbing. I let her leave class for a minute to compose herself, and another student asked,

"Why is she crying?"

"Why aren't we?" I wondered.

The day after the Virginia Tech shootings, Cormac McCarthy won the Pulitzer Prize for his apocalyptic novel *The Road*. I read it a few months ago. It's about a nameless father and son pursued by cannibalistic drifters moving across an American landscape that has been reduced to snow and ashes. It's brilliant, and so frightening I had to stop every few pages and go outside to look at the sun.

McCarthy, a master of prose style, has published many previous novels dealing with dark and horrific events, among them *Blood Meridian*. I haven't read it, but last year, a panel of writers and critics ranked it the third most important work of American fiction in the last quarter-century.

"The scariest thing about *Blood Meridian* is that it is a euphoric and exhilarating book," said critic Steve Shaviro. "Once we have started to dance, once we are caught up in the game, there is no pulling back."

I never used to worry about my students' violent writing. I figured they were working out their negative feelings through art instead of through actual violence. I permitted such writing because I wanted them to feel it was safe in my classroom to go anywhere their imaginations might take them.

Now I'm not so sure. I'm starting to fear that the physical safety of students and teachers may be threatened by such inward journeys. Once we are on McCarthy's road, once we are caught up in the euphoria and exhilaration of shedding imaginary blood, there may be no pulling back. (4/26/07)

Joy Takes Work

In one of last fall's columns, I wrote, "Some of the joy has leached out of my work, and I want it back." Well, as I tell my students, joy isn't the same as fun. Joy takes work. Lately, I've been working harder than ever, and I'm starting to feel more joy.

Ironically, it's coming from English Competency, the class I dreaded when the school year began. We took 60-some sophomores and juniors who have gotten poor grades in English and broke them into three groups of around 20 students each. Each group gets six weeks of intensive instruction in writing from one teacher, six weeks of public speaking from a second teacher, and six weeks of basic reading from a third—me.

It's hard. Nobody ever taught me how to do this. I find myself borrowing ideas from my wife, who teaches a mixed fourth-and-fifth-grade class. I even took a sackful of her class books to offer my students for their silent reading. Research shows that daily practice in reading books that are below a student's grade level reduces frustration and improves fluency.

But it hurts their pride. Some of these students vehemently deny that they belong in this class, no matter what their previous grades were. So it's not surprising that as each new group comes in, there's a period of mutual testing. I test their reading comprehension; they test my patience.

Last week, they were doing better than I was. Although my students called them stupid, the new reading techniques I was trying out seemed to be working. They all got As on the first quiz.

But we clashed constantly over my classroom rules. When I wouldn't let them sit or lie on the floor to do their silent reading, they were furious. One boy got so mad at me for insisting on reading their writing journal entries out loud—no names used—that he called me obscene words in his journal. When I told another boy to go to the office because he wouldn't stop arguing with me, he jumped up, pounded on the wall, and stormed out.

By Thursday, I was so frustrated by students coming back to

class late from lunch that I declared I would lock them out. We were at war.

On Friday, I came to my senses. All year we've been trying to improve conduct by praising good behavior instead of focusing on offenders. I've been slow to pick it up, not because I disagree with the premise, but because I couldn't figure out the right rewards. Teenagers sneer at gold stars. I don't like to give out candy and sweets—they consume too much junk already.

My class gave me the answer. Both of the other Competency teachers gave them Fun Fridays, they said, where they could play games in the hour after lunch. I offered them a deal. Get back from lunch on time next week, I said, and we'll have Fun Friday. They thought that sounded fair.

I also had a talk with both of the boys who were mad at me. I tried another new technique. I listened to them.

Turns out the one who'd called me the names had some good points about reading journals out loud. Revealing something too personal, he said, could expose a student to bullying. I asked him to monitor my writing prompts and let me know when he felt one was too personal to read out loud. He agreed.

The one who pounded on the wall admitted that he'd been out of line, but felt I'd overreacted by sending him to the office. I promised to send him out in the hallway next time, so he'd have a chance to cool off. He said that would be okay, and we shook on it.

I don't expect everything to be perfect this week. It's still going to be hard. But I'm feeling more joyful. (5/24/07)

The Faculty Award

Last Wednesday we had the only faculty meeting I look forward to all year. It's the one where we talk about the Faculty Award.

The award goes to the senior who, in the opinion of the faculty, best represents ConVal High School. Academic and athletic achievements are taken into consideration, of course, but what makes it special is the way we also look for the subtler qualities—enthusiasm, hard work, cheerfulness, public-spiritedness, kindness, persistence, moral courage—that will be remembered long after the touchdowns and A-pluses are forgotten. It's the highest honor the school offers.

This year there were five finalists. Some of us knew all five; some had never taught any of them. That's the purpose of the meeting. Having narrowed the field from 300-some seniors to these five by a series of ballots, it's a time to talk to each other about who they are and, in a way, who we are.

I don't know who this year's winner is; we took a secret vote, and the award will be presented at commencement on June 16. I don't want to talk about the candidates except to say they are all givers, not takers.

I want to talk about the nature of the conversation we had that afternoon. This is a tough time of year for teachers as well as students. It's hot, and only a few rooms in ConVal are air-conditioned. A lot of students have shut down mentally or stopped coming physically. On senior skip day, the unofficial holiday observed the day before our meeting, 75 percent of seniors chose not to attend school. We are all tired and testy.

But that afternoon was filled with eloquence and emotion; rapture is not too strong a word. One veteran of many years of teaching broke down in the middle of his description of one of the candidates. He had to wait a minute to regain his composure, and the rest of us were as silent as if we were at prayer.

We laughed, too. A coach told us about a player who, having learned that the coach loves a certain kind of holiday cookie, made sure he got a plateful of them that year, and every year since. A business teacher ended his comments on another candidate by declaring, "When he takes his first company public, I'm buying the stock!"

This year, for the first time, I had taught each of the finalists, and I love them all, so it was especially poignant. I wanted to give the award to all five of them, and I wasn't the only one who felt that way. But we decided, as we have in the past, to make the hard choice instead. The parents of the finalists who weren't chosen— no one would ever call them losers—will be notified that their children were among those considered ConVal's best. In the end, it wasn't hard at all for me, and I left the room feeling exalted and inspired.

Too often when we talk about public education, we focus exclusively on what goes wrong. There is a lot that goes wrong. It's incredibly difficult to find solutions, and the solutions are never simple. As my wife puts it, anyone who starts a sentence with "Why don't they just . . ." clearly doesn't understand the situation. Teachers are as guilty of this as anyone. By June, there's a lot of negativity, rancor, and blaming.

That's why I look forward to the Faculty Award meeting. Just when we think we can't face another roomful of surly adolescents, just when it seems we've made a terrible mistake in our choice of careers, we get a stirring reminder of why we do what we do. (6/7/07)

Swimming Lessons

When I decided to become a teacher, I had to write to my college to ask for a copy of my transcript. When it came, I was surprised to discover, way up in one corner of the document, a line that read: "Physical Training: Unsatisfactory."

I had flunked swimming.

The main library at my alma mater is named after Harry Elkins Widener, a student who drowned when the *Titanic* went down in 1912. His mother gave the university the money for the library but attached a condition: all students must be able to swim 50 yards.

I recall jumping in the pool, turning over on my back, and beginning my leisurely frog backstroke. The guy who was running the test yelled something at me. I think it was, "Wrong stroke!" So I turned over and shifted to my primitive breaststroke. Wrong again. I tried the sidestroke. Nothing doing. Apparently, it had to be the crawl.

I hate the crawl. I remember going to Boy Scout camp on Chesapeake Bay when I was about 12 and spending two miserable weeks trying to swim 50 yards so that I could move up from Second Class Scout (one step above Tenderfoot) to First Class Scout, when I could start earning merit badges in interesting stuff, like astronomy.

At Camp Theodore Roosevelt, all the main activities revolved around the water: sailing, canoeing, rowing. You couldn't do any of them without passing the swim test. So I spent each morning in the baby end of the pool, flailing around with kids half my size (I was already six feet tall), trying to get the breathing right. I never did. I'd lose the rhythm, run out of breath, and panic, jerking my head out of the water, gasping.

That meant that each afternoon, while the other Scouts were frolicking in the bay, I'd be hanging around the tents, listening to the radio (I still remember all the words to "Sealed with a Kiss," one of the big hits of that summer), and getting in trouble. I broke the blade of my scoutmaster's X-Acto knife trying to carve my initials into a picnic table. I remember the senior patrol leader telling him, "Mr. Gerhardt, this tenderfoot broke your knife." It still burns.

On the last day of camp, they tossed me in the pool for one last try. I failed, but they signed my paper anyway—"social promotion," as we call it in school. They were trying to be kind, but I knew it was a lie. I moved up to First Class Scout, then dropped out of the Boy Scouts without ever earning a merit badge. It was just as well: I used to get awful cases of poison ivy after every hike.

In time, I taught myself to swim without putting my face in the water, and I'm confident that I can stay afloat as long as necessary to survive. I still don't enjoy swimming.

So what has all this got to do with teaching? I was thinking about it last week in my English Competency class, which is a lot like Camp Theodore Roosevelt for some of my students. They've all had problems mastering the basics of high school English—reading, writing, public speaking. They can't move on to the merit badges—the interesting upperclass elective courses—without first swimming 50 yards. But many of them still panic when the water gets over their heads. So they sit around with nothing to do, get into trouble, and drop out.

I've got to find a way to teach them reading strategies that will allow them to take those electives and graduate. They may never master the crawl, but if I can teach them the backstroke, breaststroke, or sidestroke, they can keep their heads above water in more demanding classes. I don't want to fake it and pass them along to other teachers still unable to keep up. But I also don't want to be the guy on the side of the pool yelling, "Wrong stroke!" (9/13/07)

The Speech

Every year in Freshman English, I ask my students to write and deliver a commencement address. The exercise comes out of our study of Richard Wright's memoir *Black Boy*. When Wright is 17, he finishes ninth grade (his family had moved many times, causing him to fall behind) as valedictorian. Ordered to deliver a speech the principal has written for him, Wright refuses, and gives his own speech. We never learn what he says.

At first, I asked my students to write the speech they thought Richard would have given, as a way of testing their comprehension. But soon I realized that they would be more invested in a speech about their own experiences. So that became the assignment: make a speech about a turning point in your life.

They hate it. Ninth grade is a terrible year for most high schoolers; they are the youngest, smallest, least sophisticated persons in the building, and the older students never let them forget it. To speak in front of an audience, even one limited to their classmates and parents, seems impossible. Even my honors freshmen, who are game for almost anything, quail at the prospect. I've had parents call me to ask if their children can be excused from the ordeal.

They are not excused. "If they fail," I tell those parents, "they will learn that the sun comes up the next day. If they do not—and hardly anyone fails—they will have learned that nothing is impossible."

In the end, when the semester is over and we reflect on what happened, every class I've ever taught has rated The Speech the best experience of all. It made me believe in myself, they say. It brought us together as a class.

That's what I tell every class at the beginning of the project. Nobody believes it.

This fall's freshman group was like all the others. Some denied they'd ever had a turning point. Some said their turning points

[136]

were far too personal to share with others. I told them the turning point needn't be intimate or dramatic. It could be the first day of school, or moving to a new neighborhood, or making a new friend.

The next step was outright refusal. To make sure they feel prepared, I devote three full class blocks to practicing the speeches. On the first day, eight out of 21 students either refused to write the speech or refused to deliver it. One gave a speech about why it was unfair for me to ask them to make a speech. They got zeroes for homework, and we moved on. By the second day, the refuseniks were down to four; by the third, there were only two.

On the fourth day, last Thursday, I was thrilled to see a dozen family members, including two younger siblings, in the classroom. The speeches went beautifully. About halfway through, I stopped grading them: I wanted to concentrate on what they were saying. Besides, I had decided that every student who was brave enough to come forward and speak deserved an A.

The most inspiring moment came when one girl, terrified, broke down and said she couldn't do it. Two other girls immediately jumped up and came to the front of the room. They hugged the speaker, reassured her, and stood next to her, touching her. It still wasn't enough. Then the girl's three-year-old brother toddled up to the front. She gratefully picked him up and, through her tears, delivered her speech, which was about the lessons she had learned from taking care of the little boy in her arms.

When the rest were done, I offered the last two holdouts a chance to deliver the speech impromptu. One came up and did it, staring at the bare surface of the lectern as if words had been burned into it. The other stayed in his seat.

I don't know if, when the semester is over, this group will rate The Speech as the best thing we did. But I will. (10/11/07)

In the Story the Fire Burns Forever

What goes wrong is often the noisiest, most visible stuff happening in a classroom. Still, I try to remind myself to notice what goes right, too. This is a story about something that went quietly but spectacularly right in my last group of English Competency students. It involves a boy I'll call Orson.

Every day in English Competency follows a set pattern. For the first 30 minutes of class, the students do silent reading. Research shows the best way to help struggling readers gain fluency and speed is to let them read books they find enjoyable that are below their grade level. Trying to read a difficult book is frustrating—so frustrating that many kids give up. Many of them decide, as one study put it, that reading isn't supposed to make sense.

So Orson sat in the corner of the room and read. He started out with *Tangerine*, a young adult novel by Edward Bloor. Students are required to fill out reading logs as they go, listing the book's title and author, which page they started on that day and where they stopped, and writing three complete sentences of summary along with three complete sentences of their own response to the reading.

Although Orson's spelling is shockingly bad, it was clear from the start that he was engaged with the book. On August 31, he read five pages and wrote: "In this part of the story thar was a fire by thar new house. That reminds me of when thar was a fire in one of the apple orcherds by my dads. But it went out, in the storry the fire burns forever."

By September 5, at page 33, his interest was fading: "at first I liked this book becuse I thot that he was in like 8th grade and his brother was in like 11th grade. but now that I know that thay are yung my whol vew on this book is blown. Now I don't know If im guna read it any more."

The next day brought relief: "now I get it the part whar thay sed thay wher so yun it was a flash back. Good thing I keep reading or I wood have stoped."

On September 12 he was on page 113 and had caught fire: "This is my favoret part now becuse It makes me think about what might hapen next," he wrote, adding, "This is the first book I've ever been intresed in before."

By now, Orson's commentary was spilling off the bottom of his logs. He was starting to visualize, a critical step in becoming an independent reader. September 24, page 257: "I could really picthur the part whar Paul is standing at the wall and its pich black out side. then two car head lights perces throw the darknis. Then Pauls brother and his frend step out with a mettel bace ball bat."

On September 26, Orson finished *Tangerine*. He had so much to say he turned in three reading logs that day. Here is his last response: "In the varry end Paul and his Dad are Driving to his new school. Thay pass his old school and his dad points out the tree that was planted in memory of Joeys brothe that was killed by lighting. his dad seis 'See thows suports thay are to suport the tree till it can stand on its own.' I think it was a metafor or whatever for Paul. I think it meens that he can stand on his own."

I mentioned Orson's success to Amy Clason-Gilmet, head of the Special Education Department at ConVal, and her eyes almost bugged out. "Orson wrote that? Orson said it was a metaphor? When he came here he'd never read a book!"

Orson has moved on to the public speaking part of the course, which may be a bigger challenge for such a quiet guy. I'm not worried, though. All he needs is some support. (11/8/07)

Playing God

Some scientists think there was a catastrophic flood several thousand years ago, when melting polar ice raised sea levels so high that a land bridge between Europe and Asia gave way, creating what is now the Black Sea. So maybe the flood stories told by the ancient Greeks, Mesopotamians, and Hebrews have some historical basis. On the other hand, the Aztecs of Central America also have a flood story, so maybe it's more complicated.

In any case, I like to tell my Classical Mythology students about it, and we play a game in which they make a list of ten people, objects, or places they think should be preserved from destruction. They are not allowed to include themselves on the list. We played the game last week.

In the past, I've always played the role of Zeus, reading the lists out loud, deciding who and what will be saved, and throwing in bits and pieces of mythological lore as opportunities presented themselves. But last week I was fighting off a cold, so when the lists were complete, I offered my students the chance to play the Lord of Lightning. Several hands went up. It was interesting to learn what students wanted to keep from our current civilization and how those volunteer gods and goddesses responded to these modern prayers.

The lists broke down into two basic categories: those that were aimed at making a better world than the one being destroyed and those that sought to reconstruct the one we have now. The former—largely compiled by girls—leaned heavily on preserving libraries and museums ("so that people can learn from their mistakes"), trees for oxygen and firewood and homes, and seeds to grow food for the next generation of human beings.

The latter—written mostly by boys—focused on fast food, fast cars, and fast women. Music was on both lists (though there was considerable difference of opinion on exactly which bands would make the cut), and so were cows. One group liked them for the renewable resources of milk, butter, and cheese. The other wanted to ensure an ample supply of hamburger.

Our half-dozen gods and goddesses (I limited them to three or four petitions each for variety's sake) represented a broad range of sacred decision-making styles. We had both wrathful hurlers of thunderbolts and benign earth mothers. Their decisions were arbitrary, capricious, and occasionally sarcastic ("You want me to save water? I'm sending you a flood! Pay attention!").

It got rowdy at times. There was a schism over whether a new Almighty could reverse a decision handed down by the previous deity. It sounded like an argument before the Supreme Court, and I suppose it was. There was quite a bit of heretical commentary from the sidelines, and I had to ask some people to be more reverent in the divine presence. It rarely worked.

I think everyone enjoyed it, and I learned something, too. The chance to play God is one of the great temptations of teaching. We can hand down commandments, reward the virtuous, and punish the wicked. We may even have the power to determine where our students spend the Afterlife of college.

But the greatest sin in Greek mythology is hubris—a human being aspiring to divinity. That's why Zeus sent the flood in the first place. It's important for a teacher to remember that. (11/22/07)

The Last Day

One of my colleagues surprised me with a question last week, when the first semester ended: "What do you say to your students on the last day of class?"

"It depends on the class," I said. "Why do you ask?"

"I just finished a very difficult class," she answered. "I didn't like the person I was in that class. Of course, that had a lot to do with who the students were. But several of them came back to thank me, and then I felt guilty about not making a bigger deal of our last time together. Normally, I'd thank them and tell them how much I would miss them and offer them help with any math classes they'd have in the future. But with this group, it wasn't in my heart."

I knew exactly how that felt. I didn't like the kind of person I was in English Competency this year, either. On my last day in that class, instead of shaking hands with each student at the door, I just let them leave.

English Competency was a long shot from its beginnings in the fall of 2006. The idea was to use teams of educators to teach the basics of English—reading, writing, and speaking—to students who need extra help. Kim Maleski, Ann Moller, and I tried every technique we could find or invent to make it work. We went to special workshops to acquire new skills; we met every day in our prep block after class to share information and ideas.

We had some successes. In my three reading groups, the average score on a state reading test rose 16 to 27 percent. I wrote recently about Orson, the boy who'd never completed a book, who caught fire when given the time and encouragement to read something he liked rather than something assigned. Ann told me last week Orson had gotten a 90 on his final exam in her writing unit.

But more often, our daily get-togethers were devoted to venting or post-mortems. We usually spent the first ten minutes writing out disciplinary referrals and telling horror stories.

For every Orson there were half a dozen saboteurs, con artists, prima donnas—the kind of students teachers call community killers, who can take a whole class hostage with their personal dramas. Every day was a battle. We won't be offering English Competency next year.

It happens. Teaching is like baseball; you fail more often than you succeed. The difference, I suppose, is that in baseball your failures are obvious. When you strike out, or the manager pulls you from the mound, you walk back to the dugout alone.

In teaching, the failures are less public, and they're not only yours. Children don't learn from just teachers. They learn from parents, siblings, peers, TV, video games, movies, the internet, friends, the whole world they live in. If it takes a village to raise a child, it also takes a village to ruin one. Often, when we learn what the rest of a difficult student's life is like, we marvel that he or she gets up each morning and comes to school.

What teachers tell themselves in order to get up and go to school each morning is this: Maybe I can plant a seed. Maybe that student is going to take something away from this class that I can't see right now, that he or she can't see right now. That seed may lie dormant for years, but one day it may sprout.

Sometimes you see a glint of that possibility. Every day, I gave my Competency students a writing prompt, a jump-start for the imagination. One of them was this: write about a time you lost faith in someone or something.

A boy I'd clashed with regularly started his response with a predictable rant against authority. But about halfway down the page, he took a different slant: "I've lost a lot of faith in myself as well," he wrote. "With how school has been going and classes, I've developed an office life right in front of my eyes that I hate and want to go away."

[143]

I'm experienced enough to know that all successes in this crazy job are provisional; this guy might spend most of next semester in the office, too. But maybe not. And maybe on the last day of classes in June, I can shake everyone's hand. (1/31/08)

Valentine's Day

A long time ago, in a galaxy far, far away, I watched a friend of mine offer a Valentine to a girl in class. We were in sixth grade. I immediately sang out, "Bobby gave Sharon a Val-en-tine!" Bobby blushed, Sharon ran away, and Miss Conroy landed on me with both feet.

"I can't believe it," she scolded. "You, of all people! I never would have believed you would be so cruel!"

I felt bad. She was my favorite teacher. But there was something she didn't know, something I couldn't possibly tell her to excuse myself. Sharon was the girl I was crazy about, but I was too shy to give her a Valentine. When I saw her take that card from Bobby, it about broke my heart. So I did something shameful.

When I see cruel, shameful, and often outright bizarre behavior at ConVal, I try to remember that it might be the result of a broken heart. "Here's much to do with hate," says Romeo, looking at the bloodstains on the streets of Verona after a brawl between the Montagues and the Capulets, "but more with love."

Sound overdramatic? My first year, I had to break up a fight that started because one boy had said some bad things about another boy's girlfriend. When I came upon the scene, the second boy had the first in a chokehold and was calmly strangling him. Chet Bowles and I grabbed the strangler's arm and managed to pull it off his victim's throat—he was a big guy—then we tackled him as he tried to run away. It took both of us to hold him down until reinforcements arrived.

Last fall I found another boy weaving down the hall, bleeding from the mouth. I managed to herd him down to the nurse's office for treatment, though he swore at me all the way. When I got back to class, I learned he'd been walking beside the girl who broke up with him, whispering filthy words to her, until she finally popped him.

There are less violent manifestations of love, too, though the emotional toll can be just as devastating. I have no doubt that some-time today, as the chocolate roses are delivered to classrooms and heaps of floral arrangements pile up in the main office, there will be girls crying in the restrooms and guys punching walls because they got nothing.

This is not to mention the public displays of affection. We do not attempt to ban such displays but ask our students to express affection appropriately. I'm not exaggerating when I say some of them are more appropriate to the departure of the Sixth Fleet from Naples than the break between second and third block.

I'm not against love. I see boys and girls walking hand in hand, and the light in their faces warms my heart, too. Sometimes we gossip in the teachers' room about new matches of which we approve. It's great to see a girl who, because she's so smart or energetic, has scared off most boys, finally land some fellow who seems dazed by his good luck. It's just as nice to see a boy who's been shot down more times than Snoopy suddenly doing victory rolls over the aerodrome. Love is a necessity, and it's so much more powerful than anything we teachers have to offer that, when it wallops some kid in the chops, all we can do is wait for the dust to settle.

So I apologize, Bobby. Sharon, I wish I'd had the guts to give you a Valentine myself. And Miss Conroy, bless your heart, I'm sorry I disappointed you, but even the best-behaved kid in class is still just a kid. Let's not forget that. (2/14/08)

Ritual and Remembrance

It was an odd collection of items on the floor of Room 215B: a white feather, two hand-carved wooden spoons, a handsome rep tie, a deck of cards, a soccer team picture, a baseball jersey, a World War II belt buckle bearing a swastika and the words "Gott Mit Uns" ("God with Us"), a pin in the shape of a soccer ball, a novel, and an assortment of photographs. We were sitting around the pile of stuff, the members of my Modern Literature course and I. The lights were turned off.

We were engaged in an activity I call Ritual and Remembrance. It comes out of our reading of Tim O'Brien's great Vietnam novel *The Things They Carried*. The last chapter in his book is called "The Lives of the Dead," in which he explains that, while people may die, lives can always be saved through stories. I had invited my students to bring in objects connected with loved ones who had died. We were going to try to save their lives by telling stories about them.

The first time I tried this, several years ago, I had asked my students to talk about the characters who died in the novels and plays we had read. One of my students asked, "Can we talk about real people?" I said, "Sure." In the end, every single student chose to talk about a real person. When it was over, we were silent until the bell rang. Later, one of those students said to me, "It was so strange to go from that to lunch. I couldn't even talk to my friends."

This year's class put their own spin on the assignment. One girl asked if the loved ones had to be human beings—were pets acceptable? I said, "Sure." It was she who put the white feather on the floor and told us a harrowing tale of how all her pet ducks had been slaughtered by an unknown predator. She had loved those ducks, she said. There were times when she'd thought they were her only friends.

The jersey, the team photo, and the soccer pin belonged to three boys who talked about Steve Record, the Conant student who died

[147]

in an auto accident over the winter. One had played on a team with him, and two had played against him. They talked about what a great teammate he was, what a fierce but sportsmanlike adversary.

One girl brought the deck of cards to honor McMurphy, the hero of Ken Kesey's novel *One Flew Over the Cuckoo's Nest.* She'd never lost anyone close to her, she explained, but she admired Mac's generous spirit.

The Nazi belt buckle turned out to be a keepsake from a grandfather who served in the Big War. The tie was a gift from a beloved uncle. The wooden spoons had been carved by a grandfather who called them "love spoons" and gave them to everyone he loved. The novel was my contribution, in memory of my friend John Pierce, with whom I worked every day for 23 years at *Yankee.*

The exercise was voluntary, and not every student chose to participate. I was prepared for the possibility that no one would risk it, but this is an amazing group of young people, courageous and kind. No one laughed when the girl cried over her ducks. When another student broke down talking about a family crisis, the girl sitting next to her rubbed her shoulder.

A few days later, in the reflective essay I require every two weeks, everyone wrote about Ritual and Remembrance. The girl who opened up about her family drew special praise, as did many others. Most gratifying, to me, were the responses from students who said they didn't participate because they were too shy, but now wished that they had. One boy wrote, "This is not the sort of thing I expect to happen in school. It ought to happen more often." (5/8/08)

What's So Great About Respect?

We had an interesting discussion about respect in one of my classes a few weeks ago. It actually started as a discussion of swearing.

"Why do teachers get so upset about swearing?" one of my students asked. (I'm reporting the following conversation as I remember it. It's not verbatim.)

"Well, I can't speak for all teachers," I said, "but I think of it as a kind of air pollution. This school is my workplace. I need to be able to breathe."

"But why do teachers write people up for swearing?" he persisted.

"We don't, or at least, I don't," I said. "If I hear somebody using foul language in the hall, I ask that person to stop. The only time I've ever written anyone up for swearing was when he or she was swearing at me. That's against the rules."

"Why? Why should teachers be different from students?"

"Swearing at a teacher is a different kind of violation," I explained. "It's disrespect."

He pounced. "So teachers deserve respect, but students don't, huh? Is that what you're saying?"

No, it wasn't. But he had me. And the rest of the class agreed that teachers shouldn't deserve any special treatment. So I changed my approach.

"Are you saying that teachers and students should be treated just the same? For example, should teachers be allowed to swear at you?"

In the uproar that followed, it was hard to make out individual comments. But the general reaction seemed to be, sure, that would be just fine. "What's so great about respect, anyway?" is one statement I remember emerging from the chaos.

It reminded me not to argue with teenagers. But it was also deeply troubling. A lot of our students don't understand respect, and if you look at our popular culture, that's not surprising. A

[149]

freshman came into one of my classes last fall wearing a T-shirt that read: "If a fat girl falls in the forest, do the trees laugh?" I ordered him to turn it inside out.

"Why?" he protested. "It's just a joke!" Most of his classmates agreed with him, although I noticed that all the girls who took his side were slender.

One of our ConVal student learning expectations is that students will demonstrate respect for themselves and others. It's a fine sentiment, and I'm all for it. But how do we measure it? How do we assess it? And are we willing to put teeth in it? For example, are we willing to deny a diploma to a potty-mouthed hooligan who has met all the other requirements for graduation?

I think we all know the answer. In fact, I could name a few of our recent graduates with outstanding academic records who had all the personal charm of a toxic waste dump. I won't, of course. It wouldn't be respectful.

So what do we do about this situation? In the English Department, we've decided it's now necessary to teach our incoming freshmen respect the same way we try to teach them pronoun-antecedent agreement and *Romeo and Juliet*. In fact, my co-teacher Lisa Cochran and I are about to try teaching respect through *Romeo and Juliet*. It is, after all, a tragedy that begins with an act of ordinary, everyday disrespect—a couple of servants for one family start calling the servants of another family names. One of them makes an obscene gesture. Then the swords come out. (5/22/08)

Plan B

We've been seeing a number of alums at ConVal in the last few weeks, as colleges close for the summer. I love seeing them, especially when they tell us that ConVal prepared them well. Of course, we only hear from those who are succeeding, so it may not be reliable data. Still, it's heartening. But the most remarkable encounter I've had with a former student this spring happened about a month ago, and it was a student who didn't go to college.

Actually, I don't think I ever had Josh in a classroom. He was in my advisory, a group that meets for ten minutes four mornings a week (30 minutes on Tuesdays) to have a snack, chat with friends, and ignore the announcements. In theory, advisory provides students with an opportunity to get to know a sympathetic adult on a nonacademic basis, so advisors stick with the same group of students from freshman year to graduation.

In practice, the success rate varies. Some advisories bond tightly with their advisors. Mine never has, which is probably my fault. I've always been skeptical of my ability to influence young people I see for ten minutes a day, and I have had some rough characters in my group. Josh was one of them.

Josh wasn't good at most of the skills we try to teach our students. He was good at hitting people. He was always hitting people—not in a brutal way, but just popping a jab off a shoulder or giving somebody an affectionate shove into a locker. When I objected to this, Josh would look surprised and say, "He's my friend, Mr. Clark!" And the victim, if he knew what was good for him, would agree. So Josh spent a lot of time in the office or on suspension.

Once we had a fire drill during advisory, and Josh was, as usual, punching anything that moved. We were out in the parking lot, so I directed him to stand by himself between two cars. "Look carefully at the space you're in, Josh," I said. "It's just about the dimensions of a prison cell. If you keep up with Plan A, which for you is hitting people, you're going to end up in a space just like this one for quite a long time. You need a Plan B."

Josh listened with interest—he was, in spite of everything, a good kid. And for the next couple of years, in advisory or in the halls, when I sensed his marauding instincts coming to the surface, I would look at him and say, "Plan B." He'd grin and say, "Right, Mr. Clark!"

Last fall, Josh abruptly left ConVal. He told me he was going into Job Corps in Vermont. I wished him good luck and reminded him about Plan B. Then I didn't think about him for a while.

Josh sent me an email a couple of months later. He said he was doing well, becoming a licensed arborist—someone who takes care of trees. He also thanked me and said Plan B was working.

I replied with congratulations and encouragement and asked him to stop by some time when he got a chance. When he showed up, I hardly recognized him. He stood tall and straight and still—in school he was always bobbing and weaving. We talked for a few minutes, then he said he wanted to go meet some friends. "I want to tell them about Job Corps," he said seriously. "I think it would do them a lot of good."

Father Flanagan, the founder of Boy's Town, is supposed to have said there's no such thing as a bad boy. I don't agree. I've met some very bad boys at ConVal, who may well end up in that space between the cars. But what happened to Josh makes me feel a little more hopeful about them. (6/5/08)

Alarm

The fire alarm went off at ConVal at 9:30 a.m. on Tuesday, June 24. Classes had ended the Friday before, and most students who missed finals had taken their makeup exams the day before, but there were some incoming ninth-graders who were taking the test to qualify for Freshman Honors English, so the deafening buzzers and flashing lights must have been a shock.

I was deep in the book storage room counting copies of *Huckleberry Finn*, so the noise was diminished but still distracting. We'd been warned earlier that the alarms would be tested this morning. The last fire drill of the year, people in some parts of the school couldn't hear them. I was in Room 219, for example, showing my Mythology students a film, when a boy who'd gone out to the bathroom came back and said, "I think there's a fire drill going on."

Anyway, when the testing began, we all tried to go on with our business. It was hard, though. Those buzzers are designed to be intolerable, to make you want to leave the building. After the din had lasted for about five minutes, I walked up to the main office to see if there was a problem. All the folks in there had their hands over their ears, so when I shouted a question, they just shrugged. I went back to the book room, the quietest place I could find.

The alarms shrilled for 18 unbroken minutes by my watch. When they stopped, our ears continued ringing for a while. About the time everything returned to normal, the alarms came on again. They went on and off intermittently for the rest of the morning. After a while, we stopped noticing them.

That was when I realized it was a perfect metaphor for a public school teacher's life. All hell was breaking loose. The alarm system was "announcing ruin like a town crier in Pompeii," as Dylan Thomas put it in one of his poems—but we all just went on working. We knew the building wasn't really on fire. We knew that asking why the alarms couldn't be tested the next day, when most of us wouldn't be there, would be futile. Lots of things don't make sense in public schools. We come to work expecting a certain level of chaos; schools are filled with kids. If you spent your working day in a constant state of alarm or outrage, you'd go nuts.

So you put your head down and go on. The day before, we were all supposed to complete a computer survey on PBIS, the new approach to managing student behavior we've been trying to implement for the last two or three years. Hardly anyone succeeded because thunderstorms played havoc with our computers. By some miracle, I got on line and did the survey, but it was a frustrating experience because I didn't know the answer to many of the questions. I did it anyway, to get it off my desk. "That's what teachers do nowadays," one of my colleagues said. "We fill out forms."

I had the same reaction to another survey we had to do recently. This one was designed to evaluate the school system's approach to teaching literacy, and it came in two parts. The first part was short, but the instructions were confusing. Four of us finished it the same day, and when we compared our answers, we found we'd done it four different ways. The second part was much longer, equally confusing, and written in educational gobbledygook. Why are experts on literacy such poor writers? Isn't that something we should be alarmed about?

We put our heads down and go on working, ignoring the flashing lights and screeching buzzers. We go on without a contract, trying not to take it personally. We go on trying anything we can think of to raise the NECAP scores, make Adequate Yearly Progress, inspire a love of literature in kids who don't read, teach writing to a generation raised on Instant Messaging. We go on working because that's what teachers do.

But what if there really is a fire? (7/3/08)

The Myth of Kevin

Early in my teaching career, I read an article in a newspaper about an educator who started every new course by announcing that every student would receive—had already received—an A. She showed them her gradebook to confirm it. "Now that the pressure's off," she told them, "let's start learning."

It was a private school, of course. I don't think a teacher in a public school could get away with that. But I was intrigued and decided to try a variation of it in one of my classes, Classical Mythology.

On the first day we met, I assigned each student the following homework: "Write me a letter dated the day this course ends. Be sure to begin with 'Dear Mr. Clark' and end it with your signature. In between, tell me what you did in this class to earn the A that I gave you for it."

If nothing else, it woke them up. Under close questioning, I admitted that no, they were not really getting As for doing nothing. I just wanted to see what they thought would deserve the highest grade.

I learned a lot from their responses. Several didn't do it at all, which turned out to be an effective predictor of their performance for the rest of the course. Many left out some part of the assignment—the salutation, the signature, the date—or they wrote that day's date instead of the date the class ended.

Some of them got creative, explaining that they got As because they paid me off, or they were aided by Athena, the goddess of wisdom. I liked those. But most of the responses were predictable and uninspired. "I did most of the homework, I got good grades on the tests, I came to class most of the time, I wasn't disrespectful" were typical answers. Some of them were polite enough to thank me for the A.

I wrote a personal response to each letter. Most of them went something like this: "You didn't really need to thank me for your grade. You earned it. In fact, I want to thank you for all you taught me during this course. Yes, your test grades were excellent, and you were conscientious about turning in your homework, but that's not the main reason you got an A. You got an A because you were the leader of class discussions. You went above and beyond the requirements of every group project. When we acted out myths, you played your part with fire and passion, and you led the applause for everyone else. You looked beneath the surface of these stories and discovered what they mean for people like us who are living now. You got me so excited about mythology that I can't wait to teach my next class."

I handed them back and waited for a response. The good students put them in their folders; just about everybody else threw them away. But one boy—I'll call him Kevin—buttonholed me after class. "Mr. Clark, no teacher has ever said anything like this about me! This is so great! I don't know how to thank you!"

I eyed him for signs of sarcasm. His eyes were wide and shining with excitement.

"I'm glad you feel that way, Kevin," I said. "You can thank me by being the kind of student I described."

"I will!" he said.

And he did. Kevin took over that class. He was a quiet guy, not especially intellectual or personable or athletic, but from that day on he burned like a torch. His classmates could have crucified him, but they didn't. They were as astounded as I was.

Kevin didn't get an A. He got an A-plus. And for the rest of his time at ConVal, he greeted me with a jaunty wave and a big grin, like a man with the world on a string.

I started out to write a column about grades, and how for some students, getting As becomes an end in itself. But I couldn't stop thinking about Kevin, who became an A student because I made up a story about him. (7/31/08)

A Thing with Feathers

I'm teaching a course called Writing the Essay this quarter. It's one of my favorite subjects, as you might have guessed, but it's not just the subject that's appealing. The students who take it are older and more grown up than my freshmen—most are seniors— and they're taking it because they want to go to college. So even if they're nervous or reluctant, they know this is stuff they need, and we don't waste a lot of time on adolescent drama. For example, in the first two weeks of class, I didn't have a single absent or tardy student in a course that meets at 7:35 a.m.

The only resistance I encountered came when I mentioned that every Friday we would read our work aloud to each other. One girl went straight to her guidance counselor and dropped the course.

I try to drain some of the tension out of it by taking the class to the school store on Fridays, so we can drink coffee and have snacks and sit in comfortable chairs and sofas during the ordeal. I also offer to help with the reading for students who are overcome with nerves. And at the end of each reading, I make positive comments and ask all the listeners to write something they liked about the essay on a little yellow sticky note and attach it to the essay as it comes around the room. It ends up looking like a thing with feathers, which is how Emily Dickinson described hope.

Last Friday I asked for a volunteer to begin the reading, and to my surprise, Tim Mellon said he'd go first. It wasn't a surprise that he volunteered; Tim is a great kid. I was surprised because I knew his essay was about his father's death.

I had read his second draft and met with Tim to talk about it. After pointing out some errors in punctuation and usage, I confronted him with the essay's main problem. "You've left something out of this," I said.

"What?" he asked.

"Your father's death," I replied. "There's a lot about his illness, and when you first learned about it, and how it affected you. But you go directly from there to his burial. I know this will be hard, but I think you need to write about the death itself."

He nodded and took back the paper.

In the store a day later, Tim read his essay right up to the point where he was in the hospital room with his father. His voice was shaky, but he went on. Then he stopped. The room was silent. I put my hand on his shoulder and whispered, "Do you want me to take over?"

"I want to finish it," he said. Then he read what he had added to his second draft: "I was holding his hand and there was soft music playing in the background. Otis Redding was the singer. I could feel my dad's hand become colder and stiffer as every second passed. Then the nurse held a stethoscope to his heart and counted to herself as she was looking at her watch. She looked up and removed the stethoscope from his chest and pronounced him dead at 11:28 a.m."

Eyes were glistening all over the room when he finished, and we gave him a big round of applause. It was good writing and great courage, an act of profound trust. Just as important, it was leadership. After Tim, all of the students read their essays without complaint—how could they not?

(9/11/08)

Loneliness

We have a new member of the ConVal English Department. Her name is Katie Sullivan, she's fresh out of Keene State, and she's going to be a terrific teacher. But four days into her career, as we were eating lunch, she looked up with a drawn face and said, "I don't know why I feel so afraid every day."

I said, "I know exactly how you feel."

Teaching gets easier the more you do it, but it never gets easy. I've been doing it for nine years now, so I've gotten past the hump: half of all new teachers are out of the profession after five years. I don't have paralyzing anxiety attacks—well, not as many as I used to. When we all came into the English office the first day students came back, my friend Ann Moller asked, "Who was up the earliest this morning?" I was the winner: 2:45 a.m.

Still, I'm not losing sleep and losing weight the way I did in my first year, when there were betting pools at ConVal on when I would quit. But when people outside teaching ask me how much longer I plan to do this job, I shrug and say I don't know. I have to work one more year before I'm fully vested in the retirement system, and I'm not eligible for full Social Security until 2016, so I'm probably going to teach between one and eight more years.

On the other hand, I can imagine quitting next week. Or, depending on what happens in class tomorrow, I can see myself going on into my 70s. I don't think most other jobs are like that. I know teaching is not the most stressful job there is—my father was a car salesman, and he suffered plenty of doubts and anxieties during dry spells.

There's a degree of job security in teaching (now that I have those nine years seniority), especially in hard economic times: Schools don't close like factories, machines can't inspire kids to love Shakespeare or calculus or marine biology (not yet, anyway), and teaching is not likely to be outsourced to India anytime soon. The medical insurance is first-class, better than I had at *Yankee*. The pay isn't as good, and working without a contract feels demeaning, but there are much harder ways to make a living.

Our recent discussions of professional learning communities have brought home to me one big part of the problem: teachers work most of the time in isolation from each other. It's a paradox. Teachers are rarely alone—there's no privacy—but I think loneliness is what drives people out.

My happiest times as a teacher have come in my Freshman Honors English classes, where Lisa Cochran and I co-teach, usually in the same big room. The kids are great, of course, but it's equally satisfying to work with her, to plan together, to bounce ideas off each other, to tease each other and get into passionate arguments in front of the class. One of the biggest benefits of professional learning communities is they give teachers a chance to spend more time together, learning from each other, becoming more effective, and thus experiencing the satisfaction of seeing their students succeed.

If we can make this idea work, young teachers like Katie Sullivan should find it easier to stay in education longer than five years. And maybe old guys like me won't be waking up in the middle of the night on the first day of school. (9/25/09)

Cell Phones

There was a letter to the editor in this paper last week breaking the news that cell phones are being used by ConVal students to call and text each other during classes. To echo the great line from Claude Rains in Casablanca, "I'm shocked! Shocked!"

Well, not really. We teachers have been aware of cell phone use, both covert and flagrant, for a long time. It is this week's bane of our existence. I was at a meeting last week trying to decide what to do about students who bring coffee into school every morning (shocking!), but Lesley Perkins, our librarian, changed the subject. "Cellphones are a much more serious problem, especially in the library. Isn't there anything we can do about them?"

The answer, sadly, seems to be no. Cellphones are allowed in the school, but are supposed to be used only in the cafeteria, a rule enforced just as strictly as the ban on gambling in Rick's Café Americain in WWII Morocco. I have seen students talking and texting on their phones in class, in the halls between classes, and, alarmingly, while walking to their cars and buses in a busy parking lot at the end of the day. A couple of weeks ago, while on bus duty, I watched a young woman march directly in front of a moving bus, totally absorbed in her phone conversation. The bus driver managed to stop in time and leaned on his horn to get her attention. She never lifted her head. A fourth-grader in Londonderry was not so lucky last week. She ended up under the bus.

We know they're doing it. We ask them to stop. We threaten to confiscate the phones if they are not put away, and some students actually comply. Others simply continue texting under their desks until the teacher comes up and demands the phone. At that point, what happens would be funny if it weren't so infuriating. I have heard stories of girls who drop their phones into their blouses and boys who stuff them into their pants.

Why don't we simply ban them from the school? Parents won't allow it. Since 9/11 and Columbine, some parents feel the need to be in constant contact with their children. No doubt it's convenient to be able to confirm pickup times and after-school plans. But it's getting out of hand.

A few weeks ago, ConVal dedicated the last two hours of school on a Friday to a Green Field Day with sports, games, poetry readings, and nature walks. When one of my freshmen heard about it, she whipped out her cell phone right in front of me to call her mother and demand that she call the office to excuse her early. The fact that I was waving my hands and asking to speak to her mother made no impression. And Mom did just what she was told.

Let's be realistic: cell phones are here to stay. Think back to your own adolescence. If you had a cheap portable device that allowed you to chat up your friends, make plans for the weekend, or just engage in mindless teenage bee-waggling ("Whassup?" "Not much, U?"), would you have been able to resist?

But as that indignant reader pointed out last week, not all the cellphone chatter is so benign. Students text each other the answers to questions on tests. Some engage in bullying, spreading vile rumors about rivals and adversaries. At one school in Milwaukee last year, the principal discovered that cells were being used to pass the word about a fight after school, which brought so many eager spectators to the dueling ground that there was a riot.

There are other exciting opportunities for enterprising cellphone users: snapping pictures up a girl's skirt under the table, staging fistfights to upload to YouTube, immortalizing teachers who lose their composure. It's not Big Brother we have to worry about these days—it's a whole generation carrying a film studio in their pockets or purses. See you in the movies. (11/27/08)

My Test Scores

Last August, as the school year began, I wrote a column wishing for some hard evidence about my effectiveness as a teacher. I finally have some, and my conclusion is that one should be careful what one wishes for.

Freshmen and sophomores took the MAP (Measure of Academic Progress) tests a couple of weeks ago. Unlike the better-known and federally mandated NECAP tests ConVal juniors took last fall, which compare the achievements of an entire class, 250-some students, to those of the previous year's class, the MAPs follow individual students. I can look at the results of the February testing to see whether the 31 freshmen I had in two classes last fall have improved their performance since the end of eighth grade.

The results were discouraging. About half my freshmen improved their scores; half of them regressed. The average improvement of those who did better was only half the average decline of those who did worse.

That's the big picture. As always, it gets more complicated the more one narrows the focus. The scores I looked at are broad measures of reading and language use, two for each individual. In most cases, a student went up in reading and down in language, or vice versa. Some students had no eighth-grade scores; some did not record scores in one or the other test this time around, because they were absent. So there's no way to measure progress or decline for them. In many cases the decline or improvement was so small it may not be significant.

Looking for trends, I broke the scores down into two categories: students who earned a B or above for the semester and those who earned a C or lower. The only good news was that the better students actually improved their use of language, on average, though not by much. Their average reading scores went down. Both reading and language scores were lower, on average, in the second group, in some cases by disturbing amounts.

But averages don't interest me as much as what happened to individual students. Here is the boy who told me more than once

[163]

he was not learning anything in my class. He was right; his reading score went up a little, and his language score went down a little. The only student who attained an A for the semester saw her language score go up by ten points, the biggest increase in either category. But the boy who had the highest language use score in either class last spring saw it plummet 30 points last semester.

This is where the temptation to make excuses comes in. That boy went through a serious personal crisis during the second quarter; he stopped doing his work and his grade fell from a C+ to an F. By the end of the term he was a basket case, barely able to meet my eyes. That was the condition he was in when he took the MAP test.

The second quarter was also the period ravaged by the Great Ice Storm of 2008. Students were out of school from December 11th to January 5th, and although they may have learned some important life lessons from that experience, 14-year-olds forget their school lessons quickly. Of the 31 students in my two classes, 17 saw their grades for the second quarter decline from the first.

Even taking the unusual circumstances into consideration, I am disheartened. I've asked my colleagues who also teach Freshman English to look at their MAP scores, too. If theirs show the same patterns as mine, perhaps I can blame it all on the weather, or testing fatigue, or the shock of moving from middle school to ConVal. If not, I'm not the teacher I thought I was. (3/19/09)

Percy

My first impression of the boy I'm going to call Percy was that he was a lout: sullen, disrespectful, fond of racist jokes—the complete catastrophe. I wasn't alone in this impression, either. Other English teachers rolled their eyes when his name was mentioned. He was the exemplar of the species one of my former colleagues called "oxygen thieves." So when he was added to the roster of my Journalism class at the beginning of this quarter, I was prepared for the worst.

Percy surprised me. I hadn't stopped to consider that Journalism might be just the right class for him. He doesn't have to read silently for a prescribed time, as he did in the last class we endured together. He doesn't have to listen to me drone on about the protagonist, the antagonist, and the theme. He gets to leave the room and wander the halls, looking for story ideas, talking to students and teachers. He's free as long as he doesn't disrupt other classes, and so far he's managed his freedom well.

But first impressions are hard to shake, and last week I did Percy an injustice.

Last Wednesday, two African men named Ishmael Beah and Alusine Kamara came to ConVal to talk about child soldiers. My journalists normally hold a press conference every Wednesday afternoon, but I brought them down to the Lucy Hurlin Theatre to hear Mr. Beah and Mr. Kamara instead. When we got there, I sat down next to Percy. I was still thinking of him as the old Percy, and I wanted to keep an eye on him.

Percy immediately got up and crossed the aisle to sit next to a pretty girl (a decision that, in retrospect, seems eminently sensible). I asked him to come back to his old seat. He asked why. I repeated the request. He asked why again. I told him to come back to his seat or go to in-school suspension.

He blew up. "I'll go by myself," he barked, and stalked out of the theater. I was close behind, already regretting my words. By the time I caught up with him in the hallway, he was still fuming, and he let me have it. But he didn't swear at me, as he might have done even a few months ago.

I interrupted him. "You're right," I said. "Go back to the seat you wanted. You win."

"I didn't win," he said, still furious. "You embarrassed me!"

But he went back in. Luckily, his seat was still open. Mine wasn't, so I stood in the back.

The program was just beginning. According to Mr. Kamara, who ran a rehabilitation camp for former child soldiers in Sierra Leone, an estimated 300,000 children are now fighting wars all over the globe. Mr. Beah was one of those children. When his parents and all of his siblings were killed in a civil war, he joined the army. They supplied him with weapons and an addictive drug they called "brown-brown," a potent mixture of heroin, cocaine, and gunpowder that made him easy to control and numbed his emotions. He was 13 years old.

He spent nearly three years fighting before being taken to Mr. Kamara's camp, where counselors patiently strove to give him back his humanity. It was too late to give him back his childhood. When he was 16, he came to America. Now he's 29, and his memoir, *A Long Way Gone*, made the *New York Times* best-seller list. It is an astonishing story.

The program went right to the end of school, and I had bus duty outside so I didn't have a chance to talk to Percy afterward. But when I came back in, another English teacher stopped me.

"You're not going to believe this," he said. "Percy came to my office after the program. He said he regretted all the racist remarks he'd ever made in my class. He said he didn't understand. He said he hadn't realized that Black people are real people. Real people," the teacher repeated.

The next day in class, I found Percy and apologized for mistrusting him. We shook hands, and he asked me if the school library has *A Long Way Gone*. "Go find out," I said.

He came back, grinning, with the book, and spent the rest of class reading it. He spent all of Friday's class reading it, too. I let him. First impressions can be deceiving.(4/16/09)

The Bad News About Bullying

I begin every one of my writing classes with a ten-minute writing prompt. It's a good way to warm up the fingers and the forebrain, and often it gives students ideas for longer essays. I write along with them, and sometimes it gives me an idea, too.

A couple of weeks ago, I got a survey about bullying from the administration, with instructions to fill it out and return it. It asked me to define bullying and explain how it might occur and the proper way to report it. I snarled a little at the interruption but did the survey. Then I wondered how students would define bullying. So that became the next morning's prompt.

Here's what I wrote: "Bullying—at least in its subtler forms, like teasing or social exclusion—is part of American life. We can try to stop the most obvious forms of it, like slamming kids into lockers, but even that doesn't often occur in front of teachers. I know it's going on all around me, like life in a forest, but when I walk in the woods I only hear the rustling in the underbrush that tells me animals are present. And even when I see or hear bullying in the halls—the shove in the back, the punch on the shoulder, the calling people 'gay' and 'retarded'—and try to stop it, I always hear the same thing: 'I was just kidding. He's my friend.' And I know it's true. Or at least, the kid believes it is true."

One of my students agreed: "The people who bully you most are your friends or even your boyfriend or girlfriend, because they mean a lot more to you than some random kid in your class."

"Bullying isn't always the same," another student wrote. "Some are small things. In fact, most are small, so that you might feel a bit lame to report it, like a whiner. However, these small acts build up. They slowly eat away at your confidence and self-esteem."

"Bullying, to me, is playing with another's emotions for your own sake," another responded. "Maybe the bully is unhappy and sees another kid who is happier than him. The bully may think if he isn't happy, no one should be. A bully tries to take happiness away and replace it with hurt, sadness, or anger. Doing this makes the bully feel a fake sense of satisfaction for the moment. But in the long run, it's the bully who will be sad."

"There are people, I'd say more girls than boys, that will not just talk to and about you," wrote one boy. "They'll find a way to make it follow you home. They haunt and stalk through internet and phone, and they will hurt you. If they're good at it, they will systematically destroy your self-esteem and friend base. The worst part is some will do it for fun. They do it to practice their skills at life-ruining."

One girl told the story of two girls who sat behind her in middle school. "One of the girls began asking me questions: 'Ooh, do you have a boyfriend?' I shook my head and both girls giggled. The other girl said, 'Sooo, do you have a girlfriend then?' I don't know if that would count as bullying, but it was very annoying and utterly pathetic."

One boy took a skeptical stance. "A harmless joke about someone should not be considered bullying," he wrote. "Friends pick on each other all the time, and so do a few of the teachers at ConVal, but that is in a good-natured way."

The most chilling reply came from a senior who wrote, "Everyone is a bully at some point in their lives. Everyone makes fun of people for ridiculous reasons. No one, not one person, can say they've never bullied anyone."

If he's right—and I suspect he is—how do we stop bullying? There's a legend about King Canute, who ordered his army to attack the ocean. Things went pretty well, as long as the tide was going out. But even after the surveys were returned and the policies tightened up and the handbooks rewritten, the waves came back. (10/15/09)

Watching Parents Read

When I was growing up, I saw my mother reading every day. She was a voracious reader; she still is. She reads books, newspapers, magazines, any form of ink on paper. (At 80, she has so far refused to get on board the digital express.) We got two newspapers a day in my childhood—the *Washington Post* in the morning and the *Washington Star* in the afternoon, before it died along with most of the nation's afternoon dailies. I'm sure she formed the newspaper habit from watching her father and mother, both journalists, read at home. Their house was bursting with books.

My father's father died when I was only two, and his mother was in a nursing home as I grew up, so I have no memory of their house. I don't know if it had books, or even bookshelves. But I never saw Dad reading, not even a newspaper. He rarely saw me doing anything else. It baffled him that anyone would choose, on a beautiful day, to sit inside with a book. When he was dying of Parkinson's disease and couldn't use his body anymore, I used to record books on tape for him. Mom told me he loved hearing my voice. But he would fall asleep after a few minutes of listening.

All this is on my mind because of some professional training we did at ConVal recently. The subject was how to improve students' vocabulary, and our trainer emphasized the importance of children seeing their parents, especially their fathers, reading. It's not just reading out loud to the children—although that is hugely valuable in the development of vocabulary and reading skills (not to mention the unquantifiable benefits of that warm, intimate sharing time)—but the sight of parents reading for their own benefit that seems to boost a child's interest in reading.

There is a crisis in reading in our country. Studies show fewer and fewer Americans reading fewer and fewer books, magazines, and newspapers. And the younger the person, the less he or she is likely to read. I see the evidence of this every day in the impoverished vocabularies of many of my students. I am convinced that one reason for the constant background hum of profanity in the

[169]

high school is that students lack alternatives to obscenities. (Just yesterday I overheard a girl shout to her friend, "F-ing wait!" Is that an adverb now?)

I once tried to persuade a class not to use the words "gay" and "retarded" in their daily speech by offering them a list of substitutes, such as "vile" and "mendacious" (a particular favorite of the playwright Tennessee Williams). "Vile" enjoyed a brief vogue—they liked the way it sounds. But it doesn't seem to have caught on.

I have written before on the vital importance of reading. It not only improves vocabulary, it provides an almost unconscious grounding in the fundamentals of grammar, punctuation, and spelling. I never learned the rules of spelling (such as they are), but I rarely misspell a word. It just looks wrong. That is the legacy of more than 50 years of constant reading, most of it unsupervised and unassigned, most of it for pure pleasure.

But those are almost incidental benefits. The chief value of reading is that it can take us out of our everyday world. It can make us larger, more humane, more sympathetic, more curious, less quick to judge. I'm not naive. If we read nothing but murder mysteries, tabloid papers, romance novels, or political screeds of a single party or faction, reading can make us narrow people with wide vocabularies. Still, it's better than no reading at all.

If you are a parent, do your children ever see you reading? Do you subscribe to a newspaper? Are there magazines in your house? Do you have books on the bookshelves, and do you ever take them down to read? As you read this, are your children watching? (12/7/09)

One Teacher's Resolutions for the New Year

Don't talk so much.

Teach things more than once. Students need repetition and practice. And don't talk so much.

Let the students, especially freshmen, take some time to get to know each other. Play the ball game, play the blindfold game. Play a game every week.

When you asked Mike O'Leary about teaching Advanced Placement English, he said, "Slow it down. Slow it down to a crawl." And when Gib West observed you with your very first freshman English class, he said, "You're going too fast."

"If I go any slower, they won't learn the material."

"They're not learning it now," he replied. "You're going too fast."

Don't talk so much. The course is not about you. The goal is not to make them like you. It's not intended to make them sit in a circle around you with worshipful eyes. If they have questions (they always say they don't, but they always do), encourage them to ask each other before asking you. Let them talk to each other. You always try to stop them, and it never works. They need to talk to each other so they will know each other better and be less afraid of each other. When they are less afraid of each other, they will be able to ask questions of each other and learn from each other.

Don't find things for them. Show them where to look.

Make them write every day, but let them choose what to write. Writing is a buffet. Don't make them eat their peas. It didn't work for you, did it? Just be sure there's a wide variety of subjects and ideas for them to try.

Use the techniques you have been taught in the last two years:

top-down webs, two-column notes, summary templates. They work. Don't cling to the old, ineffective methods for the sake of your own comfort.

Don't argue with adolescents. It's futile.

"If you don't hand the paper in, you'll fail the course!"

"I want to fail it!"

No, she doesn't. But she'll never admit it. Winning the argument is more important than passing the course.

Mike again: "I'm not a hard grader, but I'm a hard assigner. I challenge them to do difficult things, then I make allowances for mistakes." Be a hard assigner, make allowances for mistakes, and don't talk so much.

Keep on being relentlessly positive. It didn't work all the time this last semester with the AP kids, but it worked most of the time, and it will be even more important with less successful students. Look for what your students did well before finding their mistakes. Remember the student in Advanced Writing who said, "The best thing you did was to tell us we were good writers."

Give lots of praise. My wife says you should make four positive comments for every correction, and that's with ordinary students. For students in trouble, make the ratio eight to one. Praise is water in the desert. It makes things grow.

With vocabulary, it's quality over quantity. The studies say a student can be taught only a few hundred new words a year in school, and there are other teachers trying to do the same thing. Do a handful of new words but do them comprehensively. Review frequently (don't talk so much). Scaling—asking students to come up with as many different ways to say "Hot" or "Cold" and choosing where those words belong on a spectrum between the two—worked like gangbusters with my AP classes this fall. It feels like a game.

Play more games.

Don't hesitate to stop everything now and then and ask your students what's going on. What's working for them? What do they hate? Is there a better way to do this? You don't have to accept all their suggestions, but accepting even one encourages them to take ownership of their education. You can't debrief too often. If you do, they'll tell you so, which is not necessarily a bad thing. Teaching is listening.

Which reminds me: don't talk so much. (1/7/10)

Talking About Things That Are Hard to Talk About

Of all my second-semester courses, the only one I've never taught before is Introduction to Ethics and Philosophy. It's the one I worried about the most. Partly it was because I've never had any formal courses in philosophy. Mostly, it was because I took a look at the class roster and saw that some of the students enrolled are people I've had run-ins with in the past.

But I've changed since then. I try not to get into power struggles with students. The result has been less drama and more learning. Here's an example.

The first week of class, I asked everyone to fill out an index card with a line or two about what we as a community needed to know about each other. There were some ominous statements. One boy wrote, "I never do any work at home and rarely in class." Another wrote, "You don't need to know anything."

But we plugged along. I was up at the board making a top-down web, a kind of graphic organizer, based on the information on the cards. At the top I wrote the question, "Who are we?" and asked the students for answers.

"Students," someone said, and I wrote it down below the question.

"Boys and girls," another ventured. I wrote it down.

Then one of the guys I was worried about—the one who said we didn't need to know anything about him—called out a word I can't use in the newspaper. Let's substitute "anthills."

My first instinct was to send the boy to detention and write him up for disruption. But I had a feeling that was exactly what he wanted. It also occurred to me that there was something odd about forbidding the use of certain words in a philosophy class. My provisional definition of philosophy is "talking about things that are hard to talk about," and this seemed to fit the bill.

So I wrote "anthills" on the board, which produced some giggles. Then I erased it and said, "I'm uncomfortable with seeing

[174]

that word on the board. It seems disrespectful to everyone here."

"What if it's true?" the boy said.

"Is an insult less insulting if it's true?" I asked them all.

And they were off. For the rest of the class, they debated the ethics of insulting people. One faction insisted that a truthful statement could not be insulting. A larger group said it could but allowed that it might be helpful to the anthill in question if he or she didn't realize what other people thought. Someone suggested it might even be a service.

A group that up to that moment had been waiting for the bell to ring was suddenly having a lively philosophical conversation, spiced with just enough naughtiness to make it thrilling. The boy who started it hardly took part afterward, retreating into his usual silence. But he listened.

Since then, I've been content to let my students start the daily conversation with whatever strikes them as interesting. I participate, but try not to direct it, except to steer it back to ethics now and then. For example, after they'd spent 20 minutes on the imminent end of the world (coming December 21, 2012, they assured me), I asked how they might behave in the last two weeks before Doomsday.

"I'd steal a sweet car and drive around in it," one boy said.

"Why would you need to steal it?" I asked. "Who would prevent you? The world is coming to an end! Take my car!"

"I don't want your car," he sneered, and we all laughed.

It's not always spontaneous. We've watched movies and talked about the ethical situations portrayed. We've dipped a toe into Plato and Aristotle. *The Matrix* is the Allegory of the Cave on steroids, and *Groundhog Day* proves that Aristotle had it right: you are what you do. Now we're reading Mitch Albom's *Tuesdays with Morrie* and contemplating death—and love.

Maybe it works because there are only 11 students in the class. Maybe it's because they're all upperclassmen—I wouldn't want to try it with my 26 freshmen. Maybe it will stop working. But maybe it's what Mike O'Leary (who invented this class) tried to tell me for ten years. Schools work best when students talk and teachers listen. (3/1/10)

[175]

Sometimes You Need a Berserker

The toughest grader at ConVal isn't a teacher. It's Ethan Beihl, a senior from Antrim. I had him in Honors Freshman English three years ago and then again last year in AP Junior English. I told that class I was planning to be relentlessly positive in my approach to their work, and Ethan looked like he was going to be sick. He used our first writing assignment—a letter to the editor of this newspaper—to denounce such mush-brained twaddle.

Ethan has the brains, skills, and drive to succeed in any field of endeavor—except diplomacy. His brutal assessments of classmates and teachers are the stuff of legend. He's been known to slam a dictionary on his desk to emphasize a point. Last year he wrote a column in the student newspaper that managed to outrage just about everybody involved in the band program. He wrote another one for the first issue of this year's newspaper complaining about summer homework in English honors courses.

"I don't like summer homework," he announced. "Of course I like to read, but these essays and projects certainly help nothing—within the context of a self-motivated, school-free education, how will arbitrary assignments help me understand a book?" he demanded. "What has Freshman English, with our comma-counting and meter-analyzing, taught us?"

There are teachers who can't stand Ethan. I love him. Yes, I wish he were a little more humble. Yes, I wish he weren't so mean to other students—but I have seen him single out the quietest member of a class for praise. He's a Boy Scout. He volunteers for community service projects. He's a complicated guy.

He's also a passionate advocate of quality, a stance that is bound to get him in trouble. He hated the way I graded AP English last year because he thought I was rewarding mediocrity, and when it comes to academic standards, he's Tyrannosaurus rex, red in tooth and claw.

I don't mind the occasional prima donna, as long as he or she can back it up with superior work. Ethan does. Last year, his researched argument on *The Great Gatsby* was better than anything

I ever wrote in college, a truly scholarly work. I also heard him firing up his Gatsby work group by urging them to attack the project like Viking berserkers, crazed warriors who got drunk on honey wine, painted themselves blue, and charged their enemies naked, swinging battle-axes. Most high school students have never heard of Viking berserkers, much less used them as role models for writing a literary essay.

And that's why, when it came time to choose two juniors to represent ConVal in a writing contest sponsored by the National Council of Teachers of English, Ethan was one of my choices, along with Ken Martel, another gifted writer who, like Ethan, always swings for the fences. The NCTE gives its awards to only four students in New Hampshire. ConVal has had a distinguished record in the competition in the past, and I hoped we could keep the string going. I figured that, going against the best writers in New Hampshire, there was no point in playing it safe. I needed some berserkers.

Contestants in the NCTE competition submit a portfolio of their best work in a variety of genres. But the key element is an essay to be written on a topic chosen by the NCTE, which is revealed to the writers only when they sit for the test, which takes place in the spring. There is no chance to prepare, little chance to revise.

When I saw their essays, I was proud. Both were brilliant. Both were original. Both went right up to the extreme limits of good taste and maybe a little beyond. Ethan's piece, for example, had a lot to say about nostril hair. Well, I thought, live by the battle-ax, die by the battle-ax, and stopped thinking about it.

About a week ago, I found a big envelope from the NCTE in my mailbox. It informed me that Ethan Beihl, of Contoocook Valley Regional High School, was one of the four New Hampshire students recognized for superior writing in 2010. Long live the berserkers. (10/23/10)

A Few Things I've Noticed
While Leaning on the Door

It was November 2005 when I started leaning on the door. It's actually a pair of swinging doors that separates the Humanities Resource Center, a computer lab surrounded by English classrooms, from the hallway that leads to the library. The doors are heavy, and they open in only one direction, so it's helpful for somebody to hold them open during passing times. There are often students and faculty members who are using crutches or wheelchairs; others carry armloads of books or audio-visual equipment. And some of our students are small people who have trouble enough moving through the scrum without bouncing off a door that somebody lets swing closed without checking to see if anyone is behind.

I started because one morning I saw my colleague, Ann Moller, holding one side of the door open at the beginning of school— morning rush hour. She was doing that because she's a nice person, but she was also conducting an experiment. She wanted to see how many students would thank her for holding the door open. She reported that she was getting thanked by about one student in ten. I decided to join her, so we could hold both doors open and I could help her collect data.

The results were discouraging at first: we stalled at 10 percent for another week. But we found that if we greeted every student who passed, we improved our yield. After a couple of weeks, we were getting a "thank you" or "good morning" from about half the students who passed. It felt like progress. One student even mentioned us in a letter to this newspaper as evidence that ConVal is a friendly place. We still do it every morning.

Last year, I decided to hold open the door for passing time between the blocks as well. It was possible because I was assigned the classroom nearest that door. Ann's classroom was down the hall and around the corner, so I could only hold one side of the door open, but it still eased the traffic flow, and I found I got more smiles and greetings. People cracked jokes about "the doorman," and when I missed a day, there were mock complaints or genuine expressions of concern.

This year I have that same classroom, and my prep block is at the end of the day, which gives me time to get to the door before the final bell rings and hold it open for the mob of escapees. Afternoon rush hour is far more intense than morning. Shakespeare wrote about "the whining schoolboy . . . creeping like snail unwillingly to school," but he never saw ConVal students headed for the exit. It's like the cattle stampede scene in old Westerns—hundreds of kids hurtling through the double doors, pushing, shoving, and bellowing about the day's outrages or triumphs.

Leaning on the door is getting fashionable. When a student wants to talk to me after class, and I can't get to the door right away, Marypat Farr-Szep, a teacher's aide who manages the computer lab, takes over. One member of my advisory group, a sophomore named Seth Myers, has become a regular between-blocks doorstop. Sometimes other teachers who need to talk to me find it convenient to hold the other door open so we can chat. I've even noticed that more students seem to be taking the trouble to hold the door open for the persons walking behind them.

I don't want to make too big a deal of this. It's easy. Teachers are expected to be visible during passing time anyway, and how often do you get brownie points for leaning against a door? It's an amenity, "something that conduces to smoothness or pleasantness of social intercourse," according to Webster's, like saying "bless you" or "Gesundheit" when somebody sneezes.

But I remember that when I started this job in 1999, I was horrified by the absence of amenities in the school. You were a lot more likely to hear obscenities in the halls than "Gesundheit." There's still swearing, and it still makes me flinch every time I hear it, but now it's softened by more agreeable sounds—students saying "thank you" and "good morning" and mooing contentedly on their way to the buses. (11/4/10)

A Moment of Grace
in the Music Room

Sometimes, with no warning, something amazing happens—an unexpected gift, a moment of grace. It happened to me last Wednesday.

Our new music teacher, Esther Holland, had asked if I could come down to visit her two chorus classes that day. Her students were learning songs with complex lyrics, and she felt they were not connecting with the meaning of the words. Would I be willing to read to them the poems the songs were based on and maybe talk a little about them?

Would I? I love to read poetry out loud and talk about it, and I have been blessed with a student teacher this semester, so I was happy to say yes.

Of all the new teachers at ConVal this year, Esther probably faces the biggest challenge. A number of legendary teachers have left the faculty in the last two or three years, and one of them was Ray Sweeney, the chorus teacher since 1995. It's tough to follow a legend, as I learned when I took over Mike O'Leary's AP classes last year, but I had a huge advantage: I'd had most of those students in Honors Freshman English two years earlier, and few of them had actually taken a class with Mike to that point. They didn't know what they were missing.

Just about everyone (besides freshmen) in chorus knew what they were missing. They adored Ray. Some had been singing for him for three years. His final concert last spring was a tsunami of emotion that reduced most of the students, parents, and staff who were present to jelly. Esther walked into an impossible situation where, with the stubborn illogic of adolescents, some of her singers blamed her for not being Ray. She was the Wicked Step-Mother of fairy tales.

Luckily, Esther's personality is more like Snow White's, only less insipid. (I also don't recall Snow White having a nose ring, but I could be wrong.) When I showed up for her first class, Select Chorus, she whispered that she had a good relationship with those 18 singers, but she was still trying to build trust and community in the next class, with a mind-boggling 80 students. Think about that for a second: an 80:1 student-teacher ratio.

They weren't quite ready for me, so I got a chance to watch Esther teach. I was impressed. She must have been sitting at the piano much of the time, but I don't remember that. She seemed to be constantly on her feet, dancing back and forth between the sections, directing with both hands, singing and coaching simultaneously. She looked like a world-class athlete playing badminton with herself.

Then it was my turn. The Select Chorus was rehearsing an old Appalachian tune called "Down in the Valley to Pray," which happens to be one of my favorites. The lyrics are deceptively simple:

> When I went down in the valley to pray, studyin' about that good old way,
> And who should wear the starry crown? Good Lord, show me the way.

Esther asked them to sing the first verses for me. She was right: they were singing the notes but not yet making music, as my much-mourned friend Pam Snitko, who introduced me to choral music, used to say.

I asked them to think about why we pray, and reminded them of all the melancholy connotations of that phrase "down in the valley." I asked them what they thought the "starry crown" was and pointed out the cry for help that is "Good Lord, show me the way."

Then they sang it again, and it pierced my heart. When they got to the verses where they call down sisters and brothers and mothers and fathers to join in the prayer, I felt tears coming on, and I let them come.

Every day, students make teachers cry, but usually not this way. When it happens like this, it's a miracle and a potent weapon in a teacher's arsenal—"We made Mr. Clark cry!"—provided it's genuine. I don't think faking it would work.

We thanked each other, and I came back for the next class to talk about "My Love is Like a Red, Red Rose," by Robert Burns, and it was just as wonderful, although I didn't weep. But I felt great all day. We should do more singing in school. (11/18/10)

Sometimes the Student Becomes the Teacher

A few weeks ago, in this space, I wrote the following words: "That's why I'm so distressed by how little reading students do now, and don't tell me they're reading more than ever on the internet or Facebook. What they are reading there is misspelled, ungrammatical, ignorant of usage, barren of vocabulary, murky, and, when intelligible, pernicious."

I was gently put in my place last week by one of my best students, Loretta Donelan, co-editor of the *ConVal Current,* our school newspaper. In an editorial titled "Facebook is Not Evil," she pointed out that another fine student writer, Natalie Della Valle, had researched a feature article in that same issue by using Facebook. She added that she and other members of my former AP Language class had set up a "Word of the Week" group on Facebook in order to continue the vocabulary exercise that I was bragging about in the same column I used to denigrate Facebook.

"I realize that this is not the way in which Facebook is always used. Trivial statuses and quiz results will never be beneficial to anyone," Loretta continued, demonstrating the "nod to the opposition" that lends credibility to an argument. (I taught her that, then neglected to use it myself. Ouch.) "This, however, is the fault of the poster, not of Facebook.

"Facebook is a medium through which society happens. Its flaws are society's flaws. It is not the cause, but the effect. It is easily abused, perhaps because of its simplicity and ready availability to the masses. This easy abuse is what produces such distaste in Facebook's (primarily adult) critics.

"Often, my teachers address the technology forced into their curriculums with skepticism. Nothing will ever be as reliable as a book, no form of communication more effective than face-to-face. And I agree. But laptops weren't invented as substitutes for books. They were invented to be a new funnel through which society can flow.

[183]

"Technology adapts to fit us, rather than the other way around. All we can do is use it in the best way possible, because it's here to stay."

She's right, of course. And I'm as proud of her elegant argument as I am embarrassed by my shoddy one.

But even before I read Loretta's editorial, I was changing my mind about Facebook. Experts disagree on how large a role social networks are playing in the revolutions in the Middle East, but all of them acknowledge that Facebook, Twitter, and other digital media have been instrumental in allowing dissidents to communicate with each other even in the most oppressive dictatorships. Whatever Facebook is now or may become, it's not trivial.

The easy part is admitting I'm wrong—I'm frequently wrong. The hard part is catching up with the world. I'm uncomfortable with technology, but I've always told my students that discomfort is a sure sign you're learning something. I've also told them about my high school track coach, who urged us to "run through the tape"—don't ease up until the race is over.

I've got a little more than a year left in my career as a teacher. That's too long to coast. So I guess it's time to get on Facebook. Maybe Loretta will teach me how. (2/24/11)

Is Wisdom the Killer of Dreams?

When I gave my three sections of Advanced Placement Language and Composition students their final exam in January, I chose an essay question selected by the College Board a few years ago. It was a line from Ecclesiastes: "In much wisdom is much grief; and he that increaseth knowledge increaseth sorrow." The assignment was to write an essay to support, challenge, or qualify that statement.

To my astonishment, almost all of my students chose to support that gloomy assessment of wisdom. One went so far as to declare, "Wisdom is the killer of dreams."

That's a powerful statement, and I was proud of the girl who wrote it. But still, I found it disconcerting that these students, the academic elite of ConVal High School, were so pessimistic about increasing their knowledge and acquiring wisdom. Isn't that why they're taking Advanced Placement courses in the first place?

There's a shortage of joy in high school these days, especially among the very best students. These particular students of mine are now second-semester juniors. They've been told over and over that junior year is the most critical time for college-bound students. You've got to take the toughest courses; you've got to rack up impressive grades and test scores.

You need extracurricular activities, but not too many. In my day, there was no such thing as too many activities, and consequently some juniors took a gunslinger's view of them, each one another notch in your gun belt.

Nowadays, colleges are on to that kind of resume-polishing. They look for deeper involvement with fewer activities—they look for passionate engagement with one or two activities, rather than a "one from column A, one from column B, one from column C" approach. That's much better than the old way. But it still makes junior year a ten-month marathon.

Senior year is not much better. Now comes the gantlet of college visits, interviews, chasing down teacher recommendations. One girl I know, overwhelmed by the number of choices, applied to 18 different colleges. At $50 a pop, that's nearly a thousand dollars she and her parents spent, not to mention the hours and hours filling out forms and writing essays. She admits that some of them must look pretty odd to admissions deans, as they were written at three in the morning, when she was punch-drunk with fatigue.

Hers is an extreme example, but there are plenty of other seniors at ConVal and across the nation who are knocking themselves out trying to get into the perfect school. This year my alma mater got more than 35,000 applications for 1,650 openings. When I got there, 43 years ago, we all joked that we had been admitted to fill the mythical "happy bottom quarter"—those students who wouldn't hurl themselves off a bridge if we ranked in the bottom 25 percent of our class. What must the pressure be like now?

Think about the cost of that highly selective college: $50,000 a year and up. Think about the college loans many students must take on to pay it. Think about the unemployment rate and the sluggish economy that many of these debt-ridden students will encounter when they graduate. One of my former students, a brilliant writer and artist, attended two fine universities, graduating with distinction—and a pile of unpaid college loans. She was accepted to a Master of Fine Arts program at the Rhode Island School of Design but had to decline, as it would have added another $100,000 to her accumulated debt. She has spent the last year waitressing and tutoring high school kids. Here's the wisdom she's gained from her experience thus far: "Sometimes I feel I was a fool to go to college."

So what am I to say to my students who believe that wisdom is the killer of dreams? I will remind them that wisdom comes not out of classrooms but from life. I will assure them that bad economies get better. And I will tell them Mark Twain's cautionary story about the cat that sat on a hot stovetop. He never sat on a hot stovetop again. But he also never again sat on a cold one. (3/24/11)

The Test

Last week I had to come up with a final exam for my Introduction to Ethics and Philosophy class, which has taught me so much in the last ten weeks. I wanted it to be special. I could have given them an essay to write, but they'd been writing reflections every day and an essay every week. It occurred to me that we had spent a lot of time talking in class about real-life ethical problems, and I felt that would be a critical skill to assess: their ability to talk about what they'd learned. After all, Plato wrote in dialogue.

My mentor, Mike O'Leary, used to say that people from outside the classroom should judge how well students have mastered the material, so teachers can act more like coaches. All I needed was someone who could come to ConVal and talk to my students. And since we would have only 90 minutes to test up to 23 students, I would need more than one. Where on earth could I find a group of wise, articulate people who had the time to do that?

Eureka! I called my friend Win Nelson at RiverMead and proposed a wild idea: Could he recruit a half-dozen other residents of the retirement community to play Socrates to my students? He agreed to talk it up. I, in turn, asked my students to brainstorm a list of questions about ethical situations.

They came up with 44 questions, which we boiled down to ten. For example: Is it ever ethical to tell a lie? Is it ethical to pretend to be someone you're not? If you could change one thing to make the world a more ethical place, what would it be? Here's your study guide, I told my class. Be ready to discuss any of these.

Some of them were nervous about a talking test, especially with strangers. "I feel like when I talk, I don't get my point across clearly," one wrote in his reflection journal. "I can't find the right words."

We spent two days practicing, talking to each other one-on-one. I gave them tips: "If you go blank," I said, "just ask your partner, 'What do you think?'" I lined them up in desks facing each other, and, modeling it on speed dating, we did speed ethics: talk with the person across from you for five minutes, then everyone move to the left and do it again.

Wednesday was the big day. Win showed up with six gracious volunteers who had also been given the list of questions. We arranged the room so that each visitor had a student across a table. Then we began.

In my worst-case scenario, I feared the whole thing would last about five minutes. I tried to think of what to do with the rest of the block. But to my relief, there was a steady burble of conversation. Students and visitors were smiling and laughing. I checked my watch—ten minutes, 15, 20. At 30 minutes, I said, "I hate to break this up, but we have more students who need a chance!"

They went a full hour in two rounds (ten of my students were seniors with A averages, which excused them from taking the final). Our visitors gave everyone As or Bs, using a rubric I had prepared ahead of time. And my students were ecstatic.

"We talked about everything from lying to Wikileaks to the justice system," wrote Trae Edwards in his reflection. "It's nice to talk to someone who's wise and has lived through it all."

"It was cool for us to just click and understand exactly how the other was thinking," Brittany LaBonte wrote.

"I was surprised to find all the similarities in our ideas," wrote Dylan Johnson.

Jorden Lowry wrote: "Beyond belief. I didn't expect the level we were both comfortable with."

Sky Stoye spoke for many others when she wrote, "It was one of the most powerful experiences I've ever had." That's how I felt, too.

The next day I got a phone message from Win, telling me how much he and his friends had enjoyed giving the test. He said they all hoped they could come back sometime and do it again. I told him they should keep their calendars open for the last week of June. I start a new Ethics class this week. (4/14/11)

In the World of the Future, Trying Hard Won't Be Enough

In my 12 years of teaching, I have seen plenty of students who display perfect attendance, spotless behavior, enthusiastic participation, and unflagging effort, but fail to learn the material. They bomb the tests. Their essays don't make sense. However, more often than not, they pass or even get high marks because they're sweet, hard-working young people, and I can't bear to flunk them. I'm wrong not to.

This is on my mind because last week my three sections of Advanced Placement Language and Composition students presented their final projects in a four-week unit on Hawthorne's *The Scarlet Letter*. I asked them to demonstrate their learning about the novel but did not give them a test or assign an essay. I suggested some essay topics if they wished to write, but I encouraged them to come up with presentations that were interactive, that allowed students to move around instead of sitting passively, and to use digital technology if possible.

At first, some of them were confused and apprehensive. My grading rubric was loose. For example, I said that to earn an A, a project or presentation should "inspire vigorous discussion and many epiphanies." Top scores would go to work "equivalent to that required in a first-year college course."

I put all three sections, 53 students, in the theater during blocks one and two, so they could collaborate with people they don't see every day in class. One student, David Selmer, came to me 48 hours before the presentation and said he wanted to change his project.

"What would you like to do?" I asked.

"A drum solo," he replied. He explained that he would assign each of the four major characters to a particular instrument in his drum set—Hester would be the snare, Dimmesdale the higher-pitched of the two tom-toms, Chillingworth the lower-pitched tom-tom, the child Pearl a cymbal struck in such a way that it would produce a bell-like tone, and The Black Man, a demon of the forest, the bass drum. He would recreate several key scenes in the novel with percussion.

I was intrigued, but also feared it might just be cacophony. "What was your original idea?" I asked.

"A diorama," he replied.

"Do the drum solo," I told him.

He went first, and it was magnificent: the distinctions between characters were clear, the narrative line obvious to one who'd read the book. In the written debriefing required of every student, David won kudos for "most inspiring presentation."

Almost everyone did extremely well. We had blogs, Power Points, videos, and something called Minecraft, which told the story through animated Legos. There were more traditional posters, games, mobiles, and, yes, dioramas.

One girl wrote a poem to represent each of the novel's 24 chapters and bound it into a portfolio. Another created a letter from Hester to Pearl, 20 years after the events of the novel. She wrote it in calligraphy, aged the paper, and recorded the letter on a continuous loop, with authentic 17th-century music in the background.

My mentor and predecessor in this class, Mike O'Leary, once told me to be a hard assigner and a lenient grader, so I tried to be generous with my assessment. No one scored lower than 80.

But many of my students were unsatisfied with their grades, and the chief complaint was that I hadn't taken effort into account. I heard plaintive accounts of students who spent 16 to 20 hours or more on projects that earned them only an 84 or a 90.

I raised some grades where I thought it appropriate, but I reminded students that "effort" was not part of the rubric. I told them I could plainly see all the work that had gone into some projects, but that it had not paid off in vigorous discussion and many epiphanies, nor was it equivalent to a first-year college course.

They were good sports about it, but I could tell how disappointed they were. This, unfortunately, is something we have taught them—that trying hard, that putting many hours into their work, is just as important as producing a quality product. In the world that awaits them, it's not. (11/10/11)

Sheep and Goats

The text for last Sunday's sermon at the Dublin Community Church was Matthew 25, verses 31–46—the famous one about Jesus separating the righteous from the wicked on Judgment Day "as a shepherd separates the sheep from the goats."

Our pastor, Mike Scott, is a terrific preacher with a sense of humor (that may be redundant—I've never heard a good preacher without one), so he began by confessing that he's never understood what's so good about sheep and what's so bad about goats.

He went on to say that a lot of us like to classify ourselves as sheep and all those other people—you know the ones I'm talking about—as goats. But he pointed out that if you read the text carefully, it says the sheep are surprised to hear that they're sheep, and the goats feel the same way.

There's a lot more to it, of course, but I'm not here to preach. In fact, when I wrote the first of these columns ten years ago, I promised not to. But I might drift across that line today, because I feel pretty strongly about the subject of separating sheep from goats or, as we call it in the education biz, grading.

When I first thought about becoming a teacher, I was still in college. I had read a lot of books about education reform, and I had volunteered in a local school, and I suspected that grading was the source of most of the trouble with education. I was young and ignorant, of course. Now I'm older and wiser, and I'm absolutely certain that grading is the source of most of the trouble with education.

That's because we use grades primarily to separate the sheep from the goats. We call the sheep learners and the goats non-learners. Learners come to school on time, behave themselves, listen to the teachers, do their homework, participate in class discussions, turn in their work when it's due, and study for the tests.

Non-learners come to school late or not at all. They talk when they're not supposed to and clam up when they're asked to speak. They rarely listen to teachers, do their homework, turn in their work, or study for the tests.

[191]

And so, in theory, the goats get lousy grades, drop out of school, and go on welfare or worse. The sheep learn what they're supposed to learn, get good grades, are elected to the National Honor Society, and enter the Kingdom of Heaven, or, as we call it in education, the Ivy League.

But that's only in theory. In reality, some of the sheep don't do so well. And the goats often surprise us.

I had a friend in high school who was a smart guy, but he talked back to teachers, wore his hair long, and revved his car engine in the parking lot—typical goat behavior. Now he's an award-winning director of documentary films.

His chief rival was pure sheep: valedictorian, president of the student government, eventual Ivy League graduate. He's now teaching English in a small town in New Hampshire, where he writes a biweekly column for the local paper. (Not that there's anything wrong with that.)

My point is that if we're going to have grades in schools—and I doubt if we'll ever get away from them entirely—they've got to measure something other than how obedient a student is.

In fact, one of the things that bothers me most about grades is what they do to the character of young people. They discourage independent thinking, the kind that challenges conventional wisdom and creates new products and ideas. They reward getting things done fast instead of right. Too often, they encourage subservience and even sycophancy.

Jesus distinguished the sheep from the goats by their character. The people who fed the hungry, clothed the naked, freed the prisoners, comforted the afflicted, and spoke truth to power were welcomed into the Kingdom of Heaven. We could do worse. (11/24/11)

Under the Streetlight

The days are winding down on my last year of teaching as well as on these biweekly musings. So while I still have this soapbox, I want to tell you about my old friend Bob, a gifted child who would never make it into a class for "gifted children."

I met Bob in the summer of 1964, when we moved into a new neighborhood. In the fall, I would be starting ninth grade at a brand-new high school, where I wouldn't know anyone—a grim prospect for a 14-year-old. But I had the summer to make friends, and I did, thanks to Bob. He was the undisputed leader of a gang of kids who hung out on summer nights under the streetlight in front of his house. I was shy, but Bob made me feel welcome.

He had a gift for making people feel welcome. He also had a gift for making people laugh. His parents had to buy his clothes in the "husky" size, but nobody teased him about it. He possessed a sharp wit that would have made teasing him risky. He also had something rare for a 14-year-old boy in those days: a girlfriend. That lent him a certain glamor and enhanced his leadership credentials.

When we gathered under the streetlight on those sticky Maryland summer nights, Bob was in charge. When he made a skateboard that was literally a wooden board with roller skate wheels nailed to the bottom, we all made skateboards. In wet weather, my left wrist still aches from a skateboard fall that summer, and I still have a couple of gnarled knuckles from no-pads tackle football games we played against a gang from another neighborhood. Bob organized them, of course, and assigned positions. He had a natural authority.

"Gang" didn't mean then what gang means now. We played with guns, but they were made of plastic and used thick red paper rolls of caps for ammunition. Our turf was the illuminated lawn and pavement under the streetlight and a few acres of woods at the end of the street, now long since cut down.

We sat there every evening—nobody played outside in the broiling afternoon—and talked about TV and sports and music.

"It was the year of the Beatles, it was the year of the Stones, the year after JFK," Paul Simon sings in "The Late Great Johnny Ace." When I remember those nights, it is Bob's voice I hear—joking, theorizing, planning, and promoting our next adventure. It was perhaps the happiest summer of my life.

In the fall, when we started high school, the culling began. I was placed in advanced classes, where I never saw Bob and my other streetlight friends. A leader on the corner, Bob struggled in the classroom. His wit was as keen as ever, but now it branded him the class clown and got him banished to detention. Four years later, I was going off to college and he was looking for a job.

Bob was just as charismatic as he'd been under the streetlight, but high school in those days was not the right arena to showcase his gifts. It still isn't. He was not an athlete or a scholar or an actor or a musician, and those are the talents we celebrate. Making people welcome, making people laugh, making individuals into a community are undervalued in schools—sometimes they even get young people into trouble.

I lost touch with Bob a long time ago, but I see kids like him almost every day at ConVal, especially in classes like Introduction to Ethics and Philosophy that are open to all students, not just the academic elite. It's the most diverse class I have, with AP students talking to students who are barely staying in school. Their conversations on how people ought to be treated are as deep and insightful as any I've ever heard. Bob would have loved it.

My friend and mentor Mike O'Leary, who invented this class, understood the terrible truth that grades, which only measure a handful of skills and aptitudes, sort students into losers and winners, sometimes for the wrong reasons.

Is there any good reason for declaring a kid a loser at 14? (3/15/12)

The Problem with Mercy

I'm feeling frustrated by my Film Study class. It's a feeling I haven't experienced in years. Since the 2009–10 school year, I have been teaching Advanced Placement classes in the fall semester and primarily writing classes in the spring. For the most part, the students who sign up for AP or writing courses are a joy to teach.

They weren't all plums. I also taught Introduction to Ethics and Philosophy once or twice each of those years, and I was constantly tinkering with the curriculum to find something that worked for the odd mix of motivated and unmotivated students who signed up for it. After a while, I came up with a solution: showing films with complex ethical dilemmas, having students respond to them in daily journals, and discussing the ethical choices the characters make. The last group I had was one of my favorite classes ever. Since that worked so well, I assumed Film Study would be a walk on the beach.

But things have a way of coming around full circle. I have some students I had in 2008–2009, the last year I taught Freshman English. These were a heterogeneous mix of ordinary ninth-graders and ninth-graders who already carried the mark of Cain. They struggled in middle school, and they were expected to struggle even more at ConVal. Most of them have lived up—or down—to that expectation.

Film Study has other disadvantages. Open only to seniors, it meets in the last quarter of the school year, when the weather is warmest and the siren song of senioritis is most alluring.

It also meets in the last block of the day, so the attendance rate is not impressive, especially on days as gorgeous as the one we had last Friday. Over the first five weeks of class, my 19 students have racked up 74 absences, 19 of them class cuts. Fourth block is also when athletes are frequently dismissed early for away games, so it's not unusual for half a dozen of my students to walk out midway through class.

Put it all together, it spells frustration. There are a handful of good, solid students in there—one of them is averaging 100 so far—but as of last week, I had five Fs and two D-minuses.

However, that only represents 20 percent of the grade. Instead of an exam, I have assigned the class a final project, which will count for the remaining 80 percent. It consists of three parts: singly or in pairs, they must write an original movie treatment; create for it a storyboard (a kind of comic-book version of the film featuring captioned drawings showing camera angles and music cues); then make an oral pitch to the rest of the class (posing as potential investors) for funding.

Clearly, it's a make-or-break proposition, so I've given them the remaining three weeks of class to get it done. I broke it down into chunks, each with its own suggested deadline, and every day I remind the class of its vital importance. After the first week, four students are on schedule.

I'm not trawling for sympathy. In fact, this is what most of my English Department colleagues deal with all the time. I assume the same is true in other departments. I've been a lucky fellow for the last three years.

Here's my prediction: most of my film students will pull it together in time. The rest will continue to procrastinate, ditch class on nice days, complain about the unfairness of the assignment, then throw themselves on my mercy, figuring I will cut them enough slack to graduate. I hope I have the fortitude to say no. (5/24/2012)

How to Live at 100 Miles Per Hour

Saturday will be ConVal's commencement, and I'll be there for the last time as a teacher to see my seniors cross the stage. When I listen to the speeches, I'll remember Sam Blair, who urged his classmates to "remember to breathe," and P. J. Clark, a skilled provocateur, who caused administration blood pressure levels to spike merely by announcing the title of his talk: "Size Matters."

But most of all I will remember Kimberly J. Costa, the lion-hearted pixie whose middle name was Joy.

I met Kim in 1995. I wasn't yet teaching, but I was about to direct my first musical. She was a little bitty girl with hardly any hair due to radiation treatments for Hodgkin's disease. "I'm your stage manager," she announced.

She didn't ask me if she could be the stage manager. She told me she was the stage manager. That's what stage managers do. They tell people.

I was glad to have her, though I didn't know who she was. There's not a lot of glamor in the job. Nobody asks a stage manager for his or her autograph. Stage managers don't take curtain calls. But it's probably the most important job in a theatrical production.

It's certainly the hardest. You have to be at every rehearsal. You're the first one to arrive and the last to leave. The first day of rehearsal, you set up the chairs, make the coffee, and give every actor a script. When the rehearsal is over, you put away the chairs, wash the coffee cups, clean up the room, and turn off the light.

During rehearsals, you sit next to the director and write down every detail of the blocking (where and when the actors move). If the director changes his or her mind, the stage manager erases the previous instructions and writes the new blocking in its place. This only happens three or four hundred times.

It's not a job for people who need to be liked. You have to bug people. You bug actors if they're late to rehearsal, or lose a prop, or spill food on their costumes. God help an actor who misses an entrance, as I once did in a Peterborough Players show. After the tongue-lashing I received from the stage manager, I vowed never again to leave the wings, no matter how much time I had before my next scene.

Kim was a great stage manager. Despite her diminutive size, she kept everyone in line. She also had a wicked sense of humor. She once coated a rubber chicken prop with Vaseline, and she kept a choice collection of porn above the ceiling tiles in the light booth to be employed at critical moments. At the dramatic climax of one musical I directed, the leading man opened a book he was supposed to read from and found a centerfold pasted into it.

Kim graduated from ConVal in 1999. Despite the ravages of her disease and its treatment, she attacked life "at 100 miles per hour," as her father, Barry, said. She worked summers at Camp Takodah and led ConVal's Youth and Government club to a sweep of state offices. She won the Faculty Award that year, our highest honor for seniors.

She also spoke at commencement. It wasn't a great speech. In fact, coming from anyone but Kim, it would have seemed trite. But when Kim Costa urged her audience to live every day as if it were their last, it meant something special.

She died 13 months later. The last time I saw her she was in hospice care, and she looked awful: her tiny body was swollen and pain medication dulled her eyes.

But not her sense of humor. Two ConVal boys were in the room, being silly, talking in shrill voices and pretending to make out on the sofa. Kim caught my eye, and I moved my ear close to her lips. Gesturing at the boys, she whispered, "My last two prom dates."

At her funeral, I remember saying to someone, "she taught us how to die." I was wrong. She taught us how to live—at 100 miles per hour. (6/7/12)

About the Author

After 27 years in journalism and publishing, Tim wanted a new challenge. He had already been directing plays and musicals at the local high school, so he figured he'd get a teaching degree and join the English Department. He did so, and each day of his harrowing first year seemed harder than the last. He lost weight, he lost sleep.

We all need to process our difficult experiences, and being a writer by trade, Tim began a kind of diary. Little dramas, comedies, and tragedies that played out in his classrooms, in the halls, in the teachers' lounge—his feelings of powerlessness, his breakthroughs, and his utter failures.

He looked around the teacher's lounge, a haven from the chaos, and saw other second-career teachers having a tough go of it—some on the brink of washing out. So in generosity of spirit, in love of exploration, Tim began publishing this diary as a weekly column in the local paper, under the title Beginning Educator. This column confronted the hard questions of teaching—the bitter ironies, the laughable chaos, the unexpected bees' nests.

Tim wanted more than anything to connect with his students. To meet them, to have them meet the dynamic person he was. To show them how to analyze a text, but also to eat the text, to embody the text—to become the dreamer of their own stories. He quickly gained a following of future journalists. But more than that, he reached out past the front row, found struggling students, and honored their struggle with utmost respect. No kid was a lost cause to Tim. And if there's a message in this book, it's that with enough fortitude of spirit, with enough willingness to be humiliated, with enough cleverness, generosity, and empathy, there are no lost causes, only kids, kids with the potential to expand their worlds and live their truth.

—JOEL CLARK